The Liverpool Overhead Railway

LANCASHIRE & YORKSHIRE RAILWAY
AND
LIVERPOOL OVERHEAD RAILWAY.
THROUGH CONNECTION
AND
THROUGH BOOKINGS
TO AND FROM ALL STATIONS
BETWEEN SEAFORTH, SOUTHPORT & CROSSENS. (INCLUSIVE)
ON THE
SOUTHPORT BRANCH
OF THE
LANCASHIRE & YORKSHIRE
RAILWAY
AND ALL
STATIONS ON THE
LIVERPOOL
OVERHEAD
RAILWAY.
CHURCHTOWN
CROSSENS
TO PRESTON
HESKETH PARK
St LUKES
SOUTHPORT
TO PRESTON
BIRKDALE
AINSDALE
FRESHFIELD
AINTREE
FORMBY
ALTCAR
HIGHTOWN
HALL ROAD
CAPTAINS LANE
BLUNDELLSANDS AND CROSBY
WATERLOO
LINACRE ROAD
SEAFORTH AND LITHERLAND
SEAFORTH SANDS
MARSH LANE AND STRAND ROAD
BOOTLE
BOOTLE
BANKHALL
SANDHILLS
ALEXANDRA
LANGTON
BROCKLEBANK
CANADA
HUSKISSON
NELSON
CLARENCE
PRINCE'S
PIERHEAD
LIVERPOOL
JAMES St
CUSTOM HOUSE
WAPPING
BRUNSWICK
TOXTETH
DINGLE
HERCULANEUM
L.&Y. RY THUS
LIV. OVERD RY THUS
J.A.F. ASPINALL, GENERAL MANAGER,
LANCASHIRE & YORKSHIRE RAILWAY,
HUNTS BANK, MANCHESTER.
E. J. NEACHELL, GENERAL MANAGER,
LIVERPOOL OVERHEAD RAILWAY,
31, JAMES STREET, LIVERPOOL.

The Liverpool Overhead Railway

Charles E. Box

Revised by Adrian Jarvis

LONDON

IAN ALLAN LTD

Contents

First published 1984

ISBN 0 7110 1183 4

Published by Ian Allan Ltd, Shepperton, Surrey; and printed by Ian Allan Printing Ltd at their works at Coombelands in Runnymede, England.

Editor's Preface

The average Liverpudlian of 30 years ago did not take a great deal of notice of the Liverpool Overhead Railway. He probably used it, but in a city which bristled with 'firsts' and superlatives including the longest floating stage in the world, the first inter-city railway, the largest tobacco warehouse, even the biggest clock-face, he could be, and was, blasé. This book may help us avoid falling into the same trap, for although the Overhead was one of the smaller railways of this country, it was a highly innovative one. It was the only elevated railway in this country, and first electric elevated railway in the world. It was the first to employ automatic signalling and the first to use all electric colour light signalling. It even had the first escalator in regular public service. Like its august fellow-pioneer, the Liverpool and Manchester Railway, it was in its day a mecca for the enquiring engineer and a test bed for many new ideas, some good, others forgotten. Unlike the Liverpool and Manchester, its original stock was so soundly devised, despite its novelty that it all lasted in service for many years, and a couple of its carriages survived largely unaltered until the closure of the line.

Charles Box was very well, if not uniquely well, qualified to write this book. He had never worked on the Overhead Railway, having begun his career in 1922 as an apprentice at the Railway Signal Company works at Fazakerley, and moved to the LMSR Signal Engineer's Department in Manchester in 1931, where he remained until his retirement in 1967. His father, however, became Assistant Engineer of the Overhead in 1911, when Charles was to take his first trip on the railway. Possibly it is stretching the truth a little to suggest that this was the beginning of a lifetime's devotion, for he was only four years of age, but from about 1918 onwards he used regularly to accompany his father on weekend visits to the line. Travelling down to Seaforth on the Company tram, his father would have to inspect the traffic receipts and then visit a number of different premises to see that all was well. In this way young Charles became familiar at an early age with the sub-station, generating station, tram shed, carriage shed and workshops, and signal boxes.

Above:
The bow-girder bridge spanning James Street, prior to 1900. Note the horse tram proceeding to Pier Head. The LOR head office at 31 James Street is marked with an 'X'.
H. G. Dibden

Not only did he revel in it, he remembered and recorded it, taking hundreds of photographs of sights long gone.

On a number of occasions he rode with the driver of a train, and he recounted his excitement at riding on a tram one Sunday morning when his father took it out for a test run. On one occasion he rode the full length of the line both ways on the footplate of the one and only steam locomotive while on another he helped operate a platelayer's trolley. He probably had a wider experience of the railway than did the majority of its employees, and this was coupled with a consuming love for it which lasted all his life.

The closure of the Overhead was thought at the time to be a sort of ill-omen for Liverpool, and is now recognised as having been a minor disaster. I have even heard, recently, a tentative suggestion that a small section of replica 'structure' might be erected as part of a new development, to indulge the nostalgia now called forth by the 'Docker's Umberella' (sic). It is a sobering thought that, despite the significance of this little railway in the development of suburban electric services, it might have proved very difficult to find the information to construct a replica without the efforts of Charles Box. In 1957, when the Overhead had just closed, railway preservation did not mean a lot more than taking some very venerable locomotive and leaving it on a station platform, and even the study of railway history was in its infancy. The majority of Archive Officers appeared to have difficulty in understanding any language later than that of Chaucer. Very few museums had sections for transport or technology, and in any case the Liverpool City Museums were still in a comparatively early stage of rebuilding after very serious war damage. Into this breach stepped Charles Box, and ensured that at least a decent record of the Railway would remain. He rescued it from obscurity, and in 1959 *Railway World* published the first edition of this book.

Copies of the earlier editions are now verging on the status of rare works, and I was more than pleased to be invited to participate in the production of this new edition of what I had always considered to be a very important book. It was to be undertaken in collaboration with Mr Box, and I had a number of fascinating discussions with him when we worked out the general shape of the chapters and went through some of my drafts together. Tragically, before the task was completed he was taken into hospital and on Christmas Eve 1982 he died. Deprived, therefore, of his encyclopaedic knowledge of his railway, I must acknowledge responsibility for any errors in this edition, but hope that the reader will realise that the vast amount of information incorporated in the narrative is not to my credit but to his.

1. Need Railway– can't travel

It would not be an overstatement to claim that in nineteenth century Liverpool the rate of growth of local trade and industry was such as has only rarely been exceeded in the whole of recorded history. At just the time when British manufacturing was rising to world dominance, Liverpool was rising to become the second port of the Empire, and by far the largest exporting port. Between the end of the Napoleonic wars and 1845 the trade of Liverpool as judged by the tonnage of ships entering and leaving the Mersey to or from foreign ports increased by some 430%. Perhaps more remarkable is the fact that was by no means all – considerable percentage increases continued. The total registered tonnage using the port in 1858 increased by 279% by the end of the century, and this was followed by a truly astonishing further growth by 1914 of no less than 54%, by which time Liverpool owned a little over 14% of the total shipping tonnage of the world.

If we are to look for an Edwardian hey-day in the Port of Liverpool, we rather miss the point, for by then Liverpool, while still growing rapidly, was in relative decline by the standards, of her earlier growth. In the earlier part of the century, when King Cotton ruled undisputed, Liverpool never handled less than 80% of total cotton imports, and in many years bettered 90%. On the eve of the establishment of the Mersey Docks and Harbour Board, Liverpool handled 47% of Britain's total export trade. As the relative importance of traffics and commodities changed, so did Liverpool businessmen change the pattern of their activities, with the result that trade continued to grow. It was the continuation of a momentum built up earlier which ensured that Liverpool remained, throughout the latter part of the century, a highly innovative and enterprising place.

There were, however, limits to the degree of innovation acceptable, and one innovation in particular, was totally eschewed. Jesse Hartley, the first full-time Dock Engineer in the Port had decided certain basic features of the Port which rested to some extent on geography and to some extent on his own engineering precepts, to say nothing of his view of human nature. During his long and highly productive rule, which extended from 1824-50 the Dock Estate took on its present general shape, of docks built out into the river from the old shore line in a comparatively long thin line, united by a road roughly along the old shore line from which, however, it was divided by a massive granite wall, running the entire length of the estate. Almost from the outset, Hartley set a pattern that the docks were separate. Coming and going from the docks could be, and was, controlled through a number of restricted gateways, and such coming and going did not only apply to the activities of intending pilferers of cargoes. It applied to railway lines as well.

The ostensible aim of the first fully developed main line railway in the world was access to Liverpool Docks, and amid the successes of the Liverpool and Manchester Railway Company, it is easy to forget that they did not exactly achieve that basic objective. They got as far as the landward side of the Dock Road, beyond which the granite walls barred their way, and it was the same for almost every other rail route to approach the Docks. Great railway goods stations and warehouses, marshalling yards, forwarding depots, motive power depots proliferated on the landward side, but few rails ever penetrated Jesse's granite portals, at least until this century. The result was that a very high proportion of goods coming in and out of the Port travelled at least part of their journey, that part nearest the ship, on horse-drawn road vehicles of one kind or another. Even the big Liverpool team lorries, drawn by two heavy horses in tandem were ridiculously small in terms of the traffics involved, with the result that the Dock Road suffered congestion such as the motor car has rarely achieved. With an average payload of around three or four tons per vehicle, the number of vehicles involved with the 450,000 tons of cotton typically imported each year in the 1880s, even when due allowance is made for the fact that some of it travelled directly on the Leeds and Liverpool Canal, was enormous.

The majority of Liverpudlians, if asked what they associated with the zenith of the Port of Liverpool would not speak long on the subject of cotton, for Liverpool was also a considerable

Above:
The LOR Pier Head station, looking South-east, before Liverpool's electric trams ran to Pier Head. *P & S Egremont*

centre, for a time *the* centre, for the North Atlantic passenger trade. Now it is highly probably that Alfred Holt was correct when he suggested that the prestige passenger trade was not where the Port made its bread and butter, but as a source of jam it was both memorable and impressive. The name of the Liverpool based Cunard line, for example, became synonomous for a century not only with comfort and safety but also with glamour and ultimate luxury. From the time when passenger liners developed a distinctive shape the Atlantic Ferries were responsible for the production of some of the most elegant and evocative machines ever built by man. It is easy to be hypnotised by this magnificence, and to forget that at the end of last century a large liner was not merely a floating grand hotel. Third class passengers would outnumber first class by about 3:1, and the crew would account for about one third of a complement of perhaps a couple of thousand people aboard. The ship would carry several thousand tons of coal, and several thousand tons more in stores and luggage. The result was, once again, heavy demands upon transport on the land near to the docks, and more particularly to the floating stage. The Greyhounds of the Atlantic played their part in the establishment of a need for improvements in that area.

The river used to play a much larger part in the lives of Liverpudlians than has been the case since the end of the Liner trade. Before the arrival of the mass produced motor car, a trip on one of the pleasure orientated ferry routes to Eastham or New Brighton, perhaps to fashionable Rock Ferry where the tank cleaning berth now stands, was a popular way of spending a pleasant afternoon. The more extravagant might resort to the short sea voyages, perhaps to Llandudno or to the Isle of Man, where smart little steamships which looked like half-scale ocean liners plyed their trade. The less extravagant, not yet in receipt of the delights of television, might while away a Sunday afternoon simply watching the ships; an afternoon of ship spotting would number hundreds of craft. All these activities centred on Pier Head, and guaranteed that there was no time of the day or week when the place was really quiet.

In 1852 much of this lay in the future. The Port was administered by the Common Council of the town, and the line of docks as we now know it extended from the newly completed Huskisson Dock in the North to Brunswick Dock in the South. Along the outside of Hartley's boundary wall ran a ''railway'' which was used for moving both goods and passengers by horse traction. A feature which would cause some dismay in modern railway practice was that the passenger vehicles were a sort of combination of a 'bus and a tram, in that they had broad wheels, which

Above:
An interior view of Pier Head station. *Real Photographs Co*

allowed them to derail themselves and run over the setts when they encountered slower moving freight vehicles. Not surprisingly, this somewhat makeshift arrangement did not remain for long as it was unable to cope with the demands placed upon it which amounted to some 2½ million journeys per year, and the first proposal was made in 1852, to solve the problem by the building of an overhead railway. John Grantham Esq. produced a scheme for building a railway from Huskisson Dock to the site of the future Herculaneum Dock, a distance of four miles, on an elevated structure 20ft high, the space underneath to be used for warehousing purposes. It foundered without trace, presumably on account of the difficulty of acquiring a strip of land of such length without leaving the space underneath largely unencumbered.

In 1858 the Mersey Docks & Harbour Board was formed but its composition was such that there was no radical change in policy. A certain amount of improvement in the dock railway took place, but the proposals for a completely new line lay undisturbed until 1877. By this time congestion both on the railway and on the road was extreme, and the Board considered the construction of a new line, either elevated or underground. The latter was rapidly and wisely rejected on grounds of prohibitive cost, indeed the nature of the ground along the old river front makes it surprising that such an idea was even contemplated. In 1870 the world's first elevated railway had been opened in New York, and the Dock Engineer, George Fosberry Lyster despatched his son (and assistant) to visit this system and report on whether it might be the answer to Liverpool's problem. Plans were prepared for such a scheme in the Engineer's office, but although both the Lysters had been in favour of a double line railway throughout, the Board had, at the instance of Alfred Holt (never a great railway enthusiast) given instructions for the plans to be for a single track railway with passing places. This was most uncharacteristic behaviour in a Board which invested heavily in capital works wherever they thought the existing trade could expand to justify the expense, and is probably more attributable to their dislike of railways than to myopia. Lyster duly produced plans, models and estimates for the single track railway, the length still being four miles.

On the basis of this work the Board sought and obtained an enabling Act to construct and maintain a single track elevated railway at a height of 17ft above road level, supported on beams on single columns in the form of a letter T. The traffic was, of course, to be worked, as in New York, by steam. Unfortunately, when the scheme was submitted for the approval for the Board of Trade, Colonel Yolland and his assistants withheld their blessing on the grounds that the proposed railway must stand upon a structure capable of taking two lines of standard gauge railway. The project was thus shelved for a while, as Lyster began to produce plans for doing the job in the way in which he had known it should be done. It was not until 1882 that a new Act was obtained, to allow for the building of a line of which the Board of Trade would approve.

Above:
Princes Dock station, prior to 1900, and typical of LOR structures. Note the centre 'third' conductor rail.

The proposed length of the line had been increased, for since the original proposal of 1852 not only had Herculaneum Dock been completed at the South end, but the North Docks had extended as far as Alexandra.

The line enabled by this new act was to be of a similar height to that of its predecessor, but was to be double track throughout and to extend from Herculaneum to Alexandra, with an extension of some 1250 yards to a carriage shed at Seaforth Sands. Trains were to be steam hauled in the conventional manner, but the stock was to be similar to that used in street tramways 6ft 6in wide, though of larger carrying capacity. The clearance between roads was to be four feet. The locomotives were either to be coke fired or, in that expression beloved of parliamentary draughtsmen "so arranged as effectually to consume their own smoke". The estimated cost was £585,000, and the Act stipulated that the actual cost must not exceed £650,000, within a time limit of five years. Once again, a period of feverish inaction followed, and the time limit expired without anything having been done.

The scheme refused to die, however, for the need for it was so evident in the congestion and inconvenience on the ground along the intended route, and the pro- and anti-railway interests both in and outside of the Dock Board reached a compromise in 1887, with yet another application to Parliament, this time to lease the right to build maintain and operate the railway to an independent company. The powers sought were granted, and the following year saw the first really positive step to end over 30 years of costly and worthless scheme-mongering.

Sir William Bower Forwood came of a mercantile family, and more directly was the son of a member of the Dock Board of 22 years' service. He could be taken as an epitome of how we should like to picture a late nineteenth century businessman. Wealthy, powerful and enterprising he certainly was, being a member of the Town (later City) Council for no less than 58 years, Mayor or Lord Mayor for four years, President of the Chamber of Commerce from 1871-77, Chairman of Lancashire Quarter Sessions 1890-1910, Chairman of the Lancashire Magistrates (Kirkdale Division) and High Sheriff of Lancashire from 1909 onwards. This wealth and power was tempered by a keen interest in matters cultural, which was perhaps most evident in his Chairmanship of the City's Libraries Museum and Art Committee from 1890-1909, but was also displayed in his writings, of which the most notable was his "Recollections of a Busy Life", published in 1910. Despite being a Director of Cunard Steamship Company and of the Bank of Liverpool, his busy life also included time to serve as President of the Seaman's Orphanage and as Treasurer of the Executive Committee which was responsible for seeing the building of Liverpool Cathedral safely begun. For this latter task he abandoned all other commitments for six weeks, during which time he succeeded in raising £168,000.

This was the man with whom the Dock Board, in 1888, signed an agreement to the effect that he

Above:
This view gives an impression of the system and its environment. A portion of the Gladstone Dock area at the North end of the dock estate.

Below:
Gladstone Dock station with standard 2-car train. The MD & HBs 200ton floating crane *Mammoth* is in the background. *C. E. Box*

Top right:
A general view of the structure. *C. E. Box*

should form an independent statutory company as authorised the previous year. A lease lasting for 999 years, which was perhaps optimistic, was signed on 1 January 1888, for the building of the line from Alexandra to Herculaneum, work to commence before 1 January 1890. He sought and obtained an Act to incorporate the undertaking, and the Liverpool Overhead Railway Company officially came into being on 24 July 1888, with Sir William as Chairman. His fellow directors were drawn from the same Liverpool mercantile circles from which he originated (and one may note some of their names as substantial donors to Cathedral funds!) and were: Robert Alexandra, Arthur Earle, Richard Hobson, Edgar Swinton Holland, Edward Laurance and James Marke Wood. A prospectus was issued the following year, and the capital of £450,000, divided into £10 shares was rapidly taken up and, indeed, heavily over-subscribed. Where the Dock Board had dithered for years with their divided viewpoints and doubtful enthusiasm, the new company pressed forward with the energy which might be expected from the character of its chairman, and construction began in October 1889.

Below:
A train approaching Pier Head station.
Real Photographs Co

Bottom:
A view from the road as a train approaches Pier Head station. *Real Photographs Co*

2. Building the Line

Before the formation of the Company had even been considered, a very significant milestone in transport technology had been passed at the Berlin Industrial Exhibition in 1879, with the running of a small demonstration railway built by Siemens and Halske and driven by electricity; followed in 1883 by the first electrically operated public service in Britain, the Portrush-Giant's Causeway tramway in Northern Ireland which again involved Sir William Siemens. Although the Dock Board was still not building the railway, Mr. Lyster had been contemplating the possible advantages of electric traction, and had been in correspondence with Sir William Siemens. While the Overhead Railway was in the very early stages of construction, the first standard gauge electric line in this country, the City and South London Railway, opened, using small electric locomotives operated on the third rail system. There was sufficient evidence that electricity just might be the shape of things to come to justify further investigation, which was undertaken during a visit to America by Sir William Forwood to view some of the 2,500 miles of electric 'street railways' which were by then in service.

His conclusion was that electric traction was a workable proposition: its economy and reliability might be open to question, on grounds of lack of prolonged development such as had made the steam engine almost universal, but against these doubts were arrayed formidable advantages. Cleanliness may have been a marginal consideration, but the diminution of fire risk within the docks was not, particularly to the south of Pier Head, where wooden sailing ships were still found in large numbers. The total reversibility of electric multiple units would reduce costs at the termini through virtually eliminating shunting, but the crucial advantage was in weight reduction. Lighter trains would mean brisker acceleration and sharper braking: on a line where many of the stations were only about a quarter of a mile apart the cumulative effect would be a marked speeding of the service for a given amount of energy.

The weight reduction affected more than the trains themselves, for it was not only the gross weight which was reduced, but also the axle loading. The result was that the entire structure of the overhead line could be made lighter. It had been estimated that the adoption of electric traction increased the stock costs from about £37,000 to £70,000, but resulted in a reduction in the cost of the structure from £585,000 to £466,000.

Sir Douglas Fox and J. H. Greathead had been appointed consultant engineers, and if there was a certain irony in the appointment of two men well known for their achievements underground (Fox for the Mersey Railway and Greathead for his famous tunnelling shield) no adverse effects were to be seen in the progress of the works. The joint resident engineers were Francis Fox and S. B. Cottrell. A Londoner by birth, Cottrell spent most of his professional life in the North, with perhaps his most notable project being the great double swing bridge which still carries the line of the former Manchester, Sheffield and Lincolnshire Railway across the Dee at Hawarden. With the length of 285ft and a total weight of 700ton it was at the time the largest double line swing bridge in the world. After a brief sojourn on the Chester and Connah's Quay Railway he took up his duties in Liverpool, and in 1892 he left his company to become the first General Manager and Engineer of the LOR, a post which he held until 1908. The principal contractor was Mr. J. W. Willans of Manchester, who sub-contracted the greater part of the work, retaining only the excavation, concreting and reinstatement work at ground level for the erection of the structure. His engineering advisers were Mr. F. Hudleston who worked on the detailing of the structure, and Mr. Hobson who devised the patented form of decking, of which more later.

The railway these men had come to build was virtually one long viaduct, with the sole exception of the section near to Bramley Moore Dock known as the 'switchback' where the track dipped to ground level to pass below the high level railway, and they soon determined to adopt a modular structure based on standard fabrications. Beginning at the bottom, the foundations were, ideally, driven to the rock. In practice, since much of Liverpool's dock system had been enclosed from the river, some of the columns had to be set on concrete blocks of such dimensions that the static and rolling loads were limited to one ton per square foot, and a sample of these was tested to 50% overload. Various features of old Liverpool came to light during excavations, including a portion of the wall of the old (1715) Dock encountered near Canning and the almost inevitable wooden water pipes. Only one problem was encountered from the past, namely an old sewer which ran directly below one line of columns for a short distance in the Goree. (Near the present Dock Offices). It was necessary for this stretch to build a concrete arch over the old sewer and rest the columns upon the arch.

At ground level stood a cast iron socket into which the columns were bolted and grouted, with a substantial cast iron bumper (filled with concrete) over the outside. This was an essential protection from the ever present threat of the massive iron-bound wheel naves of the

Above:
The movable gantry used in erecting the LOR structure.

Below:
The structure in course of erection at Alexandra Dock.

innumerable team lorries, the scars left by which are still to be seen in most of the older parts of commercial Liverpool. The columns themselves consisted of two lengths of 12in rolled steel channel rivetted back to back to two 18in by ½in plates. The overall section was thus 18in by 13in, and the normal length 16ft. Upon these columns rested the main girders which were of wrought iron, 4ft deep by 5/16in thick, with 16in flanges, and in the normal form they rested directly. Such, however, were the exigencies of building over and around existing structures, and particularly of allowing the required clearances for the Dock Railway below, that many deviations were necessary. For considerable distances columns had to be embedded in the boundary wall for the Dock Estate or in the walls of warehouses, and in some cases a cross-girder had to be interpolated to allow for the column being somewhere other than below the main girder.

A further problem occasioned by the Dock Railway was that it precluded the use of normal diagonal bracing between the columns, which made necessary the use of the robust, but shallow, lattice bracing below the deck shown in the diagram. Liverpool has long, and with justification, been known as "The Windy City", and for much of its length the Overhead had to face the worst the weather could offer. Not being free of curves the structure also had to cope with centrifugal loads imposed by the trains, so that it was plainly desirable to employ a form of decking which would add considerably to the lateral strength of the columns and cross bracing. Under the terms of the enabling act it was required that the decking be waterproof, and the form which achieved both these requirements also earned the railway the name of "The Dockers' Umbrella" (pronounced "umber-ella"). Patented by G. A. Hobson, it consisted of a series of arched plates rivetted to T bars.

Surface water was carried away by the V shaped channel above each T bar (the bottom of the channel being sealed with asphalt) to an outlet in the main girder and thence to a cast iron gutter carried on the outside of the main girder and to a down pipe.

A depot for the work of construction was established at the extreme north end of the line within the North Mersey Goods Yard of the Lancashire & Yorkshire Railway and equipped with all that was necessary for the manufacture of the spans as well as their transport and erection. Almost all the structure was pre-fabricated here, with the aim of minimising the disturbance to traffic on the Dock Road and Railway, the congestion of which was, after all, the reason for undertaking the work in the first place. The structure therefore began at the depot and worked its way South, being itself the means of carrying successive additional sections as they were completed. A further difficulty which was overcome by this procedure was that the completed sections were attached to each other by bolting, which meant that riveters' hearths, and the fire risk they represented, could be confined to one area, and that well away from sailing ships. It also implied, however, that an early decision had to be taken as to the optimum length of a standard span, and this was taken as 50ft. It probably seemed like a good idea at the time, but in fact the numerous existing constraints on the siting of columns and the provision of clearnaces for both the Overhead trains and the Dock Board trains meant that about two-thirds of the structure consisted of "abnormal" spans of one length or another,

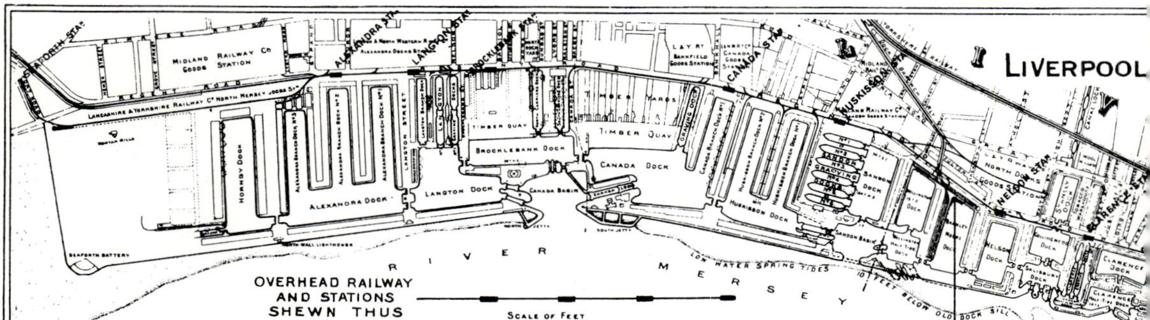

varying between 30ft and 70ft. The overlength spans were more ''abnormal'' than the shorter ones, for it was considered advisable to make them with deeper main girders, thus causing further problems of standardisation in the depot.

Most of the work of constructing a span was of a straightforward nature employing well-tried methods, but the novel form of decking employed gave rise to some initial problems. The method used was to heat the plates and then press them over dies to the correct arch form, but it was found that as the plates cooled after pressing they did not retain their form, curling upwards and spreading outwards at the ends. Alterations to the dies, giving them a ''set'' in opposite directions and the employment of a frame to restrain the plates while cooling provided an answer. The plates were then drilled by a special-purpose drilling rig with multiple heads and rivetted to the

Above:
Pier Head station on the left, electric trams and the LOR stretching away to the North. View taken c1901.

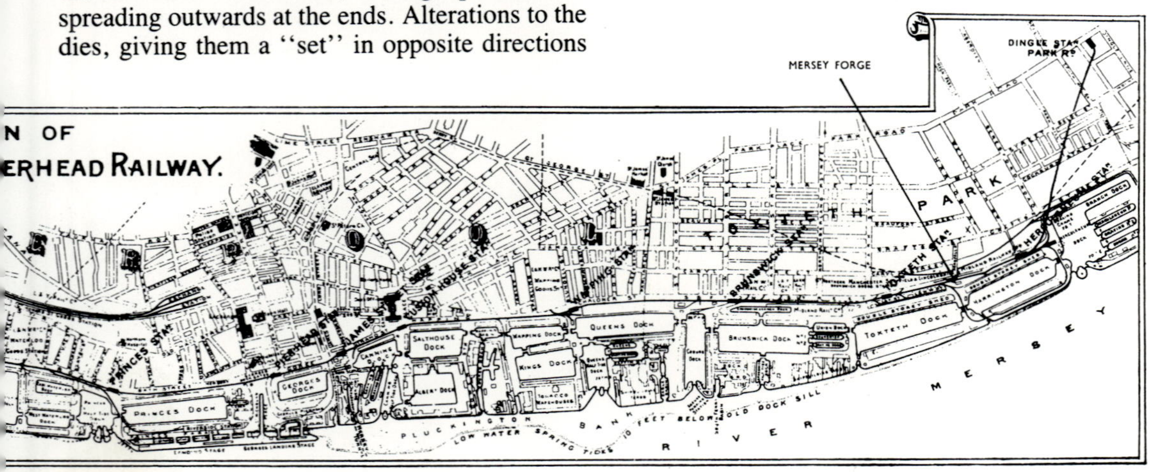

Above:
Construction under way at the Goree.

Below:
A length of the structure nearing completion.

Above:
Testing the double-deck swingbridge at Stanley in 1893.

T bars by mechanical riveters capable of closing 400 rivets per hour. As the job went on the technique became more and more polished, with one gang of men, using one furnace, one press and one drilling machine produced 64 plates ready for riveting on the final day's work.

While manufacture of the decking plates proceeded it was also necessary to carry out tests to ensure that their strength was sufficient. The method employed was to rivet up three plates together, making a section of decking 7ft 6in long and 22ft wide, and support it at the ends, corresponding to its intended position resting on the main girders. It was then loaded up, the load being distributed along four lines corresponding with the positions of the rails. The ultimate collapse of those which were tested to destruction occurred at a load of 163 tons.

Once a section of the structure had been completed near the depot the procedure for erection could be much simplified, and that normally adopted was to load the next completed span onto a specially designed trolley running on the completed portion. This vehicle had a gauge of 16ft, enabling it to run on the two outer rails and was of sufficient height to allow the new span to clear the main girders of the portion on which it was running. Arriving at the end of the track, it met a specially built erecting span, which consisted of a lattice gantry, one end of which rested on the columns of the completed portion and the other end of which rested on the ground, on rather spindly legs. Along its top ran two gantry cranes, which were able to run over the trolley carrying the new span, lift it, travel it to its appointed place and there lower it. Ponderous though this arrangement may sound when described, particularly when it is borne in mind that a total of 576 spans had eventually to be erected, it appears to have worked remarkably well. The time taken from the arrival of a new span on the trolley to its lowering onto its bearings averaged only an hour, and the erecting span could then be moved forward while the trolley returned for another span. A rate of two spans a day was possible, and up to twelve in a (5½ day) week was achieved, representing perhaps 650 feet of completed viaduct.

Not all of the job of building the line was as simple as this. Apart from numerous minor alterations to the Dock Railway, many Police

Above:
Another view of testing the double-deck swingbridge at Stanley in 1893.

boxes and other more substantial buildings which were in the way had to be removed and resited or replaced. Above all, it was necessary to provide four substantial movable bridges. The company was fortunate in that there was only one water gap on its route, the passage from Collingwood to Stanley, but this one provided something of a challenge in that the passage was in very frequent use by small craft, the amount of space on the site was very restricted and the congestion of road and rail traffic already existing utterly precluded any prolonged construction work. The chosen solution was a double decker swing bridge operated by hydraulic power and the small craft problem was nicely dealt with by providing for the two decks to swing independently of one another. The frequent small craft could thus pass without disturbing the equally frequent Overhead trains, while the two decks could be swung 'off' together to accommodate the relatively few larger craft which needed to pass in or out of Stanley.

With the aid of the Dock Board's floating steam crane *Atlas* it proved possible to remove the old bridge, make the necessary alterations to the masonry of the passage and erect the new bridge within a period of ten days. This was a considerable achievement; the old bridge represented 150 tons of scrap to dismantle and remove, while the new bridge weighed 600 tons. It is an interesting reflection on present day prices to note that this rather complex structure cost £20,000.

There were other complications. Liverpool was primarily an export port, serving the part of England which produced and exported huge amounts of industrial equipment to destinations all over the world. There would plainly be loads needing access to the docks which would exceed the 14ft or so clearance generally available under the structure, and provision was made for these in the shape of three lift bridges, at Langton, Sandon and Brunswick Docks. The rising side was 33ft 9in from the pivot in each case, and the shorter side, incorporating the balance box 14ft 6in. When raised the bridge closely approached the vertical, leaving excellent access for extraordinary loads, though the frequency of the service was such that there was no question of lifting a bridge 'off' during the hours of operation of the railway. As at Stanley Swing Bridge, the motive power was hydraulic; initially the supply was from the Dock Board's mains, but when the Liverpool Hydraulic Power Company began pumping in 1896 a supply was also connected from their mains to provide 'belt and braces'. As

Above and below:
A view from the old road swingbridge of the new double-deck structure at Stanley during its erection.

was often the case with hydraulic machinery, the rams were neatly housed inside the pivot columns, with the result that the means of operating the bridge was far from obvious to the uninitiated. In later years, the use of floating steam cranes by the Dock Board, and especially the *Mammoth,* with its enormous reach, meant that it was often less trouble to crane items clear across the railway than to keep loading gangs on in the evening when the bridges could be lifted, with the result that use of the movable bridges declined.

At Pier Head there were no less than three public thoroughfares which were of huge width and could not be spanned by the normal form of structure and bow girder bridges 98ft long had to be employed. Perhaps the most nostalgic of all the views of old Liverpool which feature the Overhead are those showing dense horse-drawn traffic around Pier Head, including one or more of these bridges, which were located at the bottoms of Chapel St., Water St., and James St.

The corrugated nature of the decking and need to prevent electrical leakage to earth meant that the permanent way could not be attached to transverse sleepers in the conventional manner. Longitudinal sleepers were used, secured to the decking by riveted-on lugs and oak keys, the flat-bottomed rails being secured to the sleepers by dog-spikes and fang-bolts. Care was needed to ensure that none of the metal fastenings effected any fortuitous and illicit meetings, but the current leakage, when this could be determined, was found to be at an extremely low level. (Lower indeed than Westinghouse could achieve on the Mersey Railway without the problems of a metal decking some ten years later.) A typical sleeper was of 10in by 5in section, but alterations were necessary in places, as superelevation was achieved by variations in sleeper thickness and check-rails were attached to sleepers of 15in width. Electrical continuity between rails was ensured by wrought iron bonds, riveted to the web of the rail, bridging across the fishplates, and at each station all four running rails were cross-bonded to raise the sectional area of rail carrying the return current to about 22sq in.

The positive rail was originally mounted in the middle of the running rails on insulators attached to cross-timbers. It was of channel section, both the top and the sides serving as contact surfaces, an arrangement later discarded. The problem of crossovers was dealt with by mounting the positive rail ¾in above the level of the running rails and breaking it at the points, the end to each side of the gap being bent parallel to the track crossing over for a foot or so, which was sufficient to allow the collector shoe to bridge the gap and ensure continuity of supply.

An electric railway was in itself somewhat unusual in 1893, but the implication existed that more than the traction could be electrically operated, and it took only a slightly alarming estimate for the provision of conventional signalling equipment to cause the engineers for the line to look seriously at employing electric automatic signalling. During 1891 therefore, tenders for the provision of an electric system were sought, and the scheme laid before the Board of Trade, to ascertain whether they would accept such a novel arrangement for the control of what was to be a heavily worked passenger line. The system proposed had been patented in April that year (No. 7827) by Ilius Augustus Timmis, and in December the Board of Trade indicated that, following detailed inspections and investigations, they would give provisional sanction for its use. The Company was thus able to let the contract, which went to the Electric Construction Co. Ltd of Wolverhampton, the work actually being executed under sub-contract by the Railway Signal Co, Ltd of Fazakerley.

The two terminal stations were operated by ordinary mechanical signals, but all the other stations were controlled by the electric system. The basic principal of which was that there were no distant signals, but only a home and a starter signal for each direction at each station. This simple arrangement was acceptable because of the very short distances between stations, so that the starter of one station could reasonably act as the distant for the next. The signals themselves were of the usual semaphore lower quadrant lamp type, but there the similarity to mechanical signalling ended. They were, of course, contrived to fail safe, and were pulled off (clear) by the application of a current of 5A at 40V to a Currie long-pull electro-magnet. Once the signal had moved a secondary pair of contacts switched in a resistance so that the signal could be held off with a much reduced current of only 0.25A. The current was provided by 50V accumulators at each station, one of which worked the station lamps, the signal lamps and the signal solenoids while the other was on charge from the traction supply via a rotary transformer. Clearly a failure in supply would release the solenoid and cause the signal to move back to danger. To aid

Above:
Round the Bends! The cranes of Alexandra Dock are in the background. *C. E. Box*

Below:
Looking North from Nelson Dock station in May 1931 and showing the 'switchback' – the 1 in 40 and 1 in 80 incline under the high level coal railway which crosses the LOR and seen in the distance. *C. E. Box*

Above:
Toxteth Dock station with the Cheshire Lines Committee's Brunswick goods station in the background. *C. E. Box*

Left:
The LOR at the bottom end of Brunswick Street showing Pier Head station on the left. *C. E. Box*

Below:
James Street bridge. *C. E. Box*

Above right:
The bridge at St Nicholas Place c1922. *C. E. Box*

nocturnal safety the signal lamps each used two filament lamps in parallel, so that if one failed the other would remain lit.

The signals were operated entirely by the passage of the trains themselves, the only use of signalmen being at the termini. Contact boxes were placed on the outside of the line, with a protruding lever which was operated by a striker board at the rear of each train. The contacts were of two distinct kinds: a 'breaker contact' when struck by the board broke the circuit, thus setting the signal to danger; a 'maker contact' completed the circuit, setting the signal to clear. All contacts were in duplicate to minimise the risk of failure.

The sequence of events as a train proceeded may be described, with reference to the diagram, as follows:

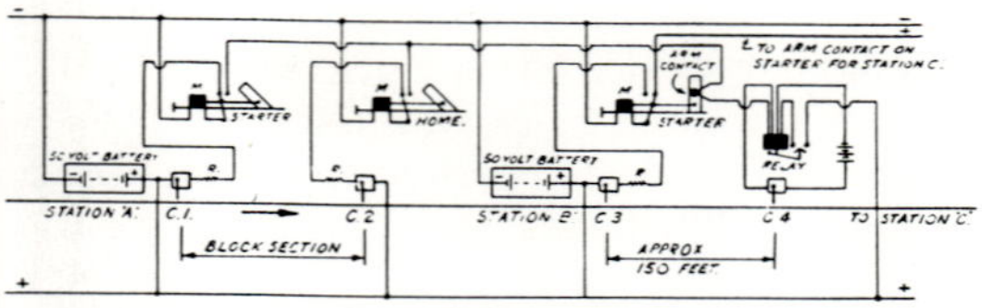

A Timmis's automatic electric signalling.

Assuming that a previous train has cleared signals by passing contact C4, the starter at station A and the home at station B will be at clear.

The train leaving station A passes the breaker contact C1, setting the starter to danger, then breaker C2, setting the home for station B also to danger. As it left station B, breaker C3 set the starter for station B to danger; provided this had occurred, the passage of the train then tripped maker C4, setting the starter for station A and the home for station B to clear, the starter at Station B protecting the rear of the train as it proceeded to station C.

From the above it will be evident that at the start of a day all the signals (having been switched off for the night) would be at danger, and the means of dealing with the problem was the running of a pilot train, which carried staff to their work. This train carried no fare-paying passengers, and ran the full length of the line in both directions passing all automatic signals at danger and tripping all the contacts, thus leaving signals correctly set for the commencement of normal working.

As might be expected of a complete installation of an untried system, a number of alterations were necessary over the years, but the signalling as originally installed worked adequately for many years, and was the first such system to meet the exacting requirements of the Board of Trade, thus marking down to the Overhead a highly significant step in the development of railway practice.

It is an unhappy footnote to this success story that when Sir William Forwood wrote his "Recollections of a Busy Life" he found it necessary to place on record his view that both the Dock Board and the Corporation had been at best unhelpful during construction and that in two instances had acted in a manner which, in his view, amounted almost to extortion. Whether or not these incidents had any really lasting effects, they left an unpleasant taste in the mouth, and may have been instrumental in the formation of a relationship with the Corporation which, over the years, was to sap the revenue of the Company and may have been a significant factor in its ultimate demise.

3. The Power Supply

The decision to adopt electric traction had been a bold one, for it was not only electric vehicles which were in their infancy, but also electricity generating stations. While it is commonplace to accept that Liverpool entrepreneurs of last century were both innovative and imaginative, it is worth remembering that the very first manifestation of electricity supply in Liverpool had only taken place in 1878 and had consisted of a trial arc lamp erected at Pier Head, opposite St. Nicholas' Church. This tentative beginning was followed by a contract to the British Electric Light Company for the lighting of several streets, including Lime Street and London Road, but the results appear to have been unsatisfactory and the company withdrew in 1882. Whether the supply for their short-lived venture originated in batteries or dynamos is not known.

There was no doubt, however, that for lighting at least, electricity was the technique of the future, and in 1883 Messrs Holmes and Vaudery, who had commenced business as Civil Engineers the previous year, formed the Liverpool Electric Supply Co. Ltd with a nominal capital of £10,000. They established a generating station in Eberle Street, where a small gas engine drove a dynamo to produce direct current at a pressure of 100Vdc, and also manufactured fittings, installed equipment and hired machinery. The initial charges made to customers are not known, but in 1885 they were charging £2.5s.0d (£2.25) per lamp per year. What is known of their first year's trading is that it was sufficiently successful to allow the payment of a dividend of 5%, and it certainly proved a springboard for expansion, for the company opened further generating stations in Rose Street (1883), Tithebarn Street (1887), and Oldham Place (1890). Despite the fact that the dynamo as a practical machine had barely reached its silver jubilee, the success of the Liverpool Electric Supply Company must have offered substantial encouragement to the Directors of the Railway when coming to their decision.

In choosing a site for the generating station a number of desiderata applied apart from the obvious ones of sufficient space and reasonable price. Plainly the station should be near the half-way point of the line so that the maximum distance for voltage drop was nearly equal in both directions and where there was a good supply of water for the boilers. More important, the pressure on land use in the target area meant that there was no question of having a huge condenser cold well after the manner of the 'mill lodges' of the cotton industry, so a plentiful supply of cheap cooling water for the condensers was essential. Finally it was desirable to minimise the handling and stockholding of coal for the boilers.

Two miles 974 yards south of Seaforth Sands station and three miles 737 yards north of Herculaneum Station was not exactly half way, but it was the location chosen for two very good reasons: it offered access to open dock water for cooling purposes, but more particularly it was the point at which there were twelve viaduct arches available underneath the high level coal railway at Bramley Moore Dock. This was a coaling system in which wagons were carried from the Lancashire & Yorkshire Railway direct alongside ships in the dock at a suitable level for direct tipping into bunker or hold. For the Railway it meant that any amount of coal could be delivered through the roof more or less whenever it was wanted.

The plant which was to be installed had to produce sufficient power to operate a three-minute service on six miles of double track. The trains were to be two-car units, seating 114 passengers, and were required to accomplish the six miles in 29 minutes, including stops of half a minute at each of the 13 stations. Simple arithmetic established that this needed twenty trains running at any one time and that the weight of a loaded train could be taken as 34ton. Rather less simple arithmetic was now employed to calculate the power load that this implied. All the stations were close together (in one case less than three hundred yards separated two stations) so that trains could scarcely ever attain a speed which could be considered uniform, virtually all travel being under either acceleration or braking, and data from other railways were used to assess at what points on the track the trains would be accelerating and at which braking. Graphs were then drawn to show the energy required to

Above:
The first four main engines and dynamos at the generating station. Photograph taken on 3 January 1893 for The Electric Construction Co. Ltd.

provide the rates of acceleration for the distances over which they needed to be achieved in order to meet the demands of the timetable. Once these graphs existed it was an easy matter to work out the total power required for the service, making a rule of thumb allowance for electrical losses. This estimate totalled nearly 900hp for the electrical supply (1200-1400A at 500V, and it was therefore necessary to install four dynamos of 300ehp to provide capacity for overhaul of one machine without jeopardising the service.

The electrical side of the Railway may have been on the frontiers of contemporary technology, but its power station represented very conservative, tried and tested, steam practice. A large (98ft by 60ft) boiler house contained six 30ft by 8ft Lancashire boilers, with cross tubes. The advantage of having a coal railway overhead was capitalised upon by the provision of a system of hopper, conveyors and mechanical stokers by T & T Vickers of Earlestown to feed the boilers with the minimum of labour and storage cost. The whole feed system was operated by one engine of 10ihp, and the boiler house also contained the twin feed pumps, each of which could deliver about 6,700gall per hour, sufficient for four boilers.

Adjoining the boiler house was the economiser room. Feed water preheat was provided by two Green's economisers which recovered waste heat from the flue gases on their way to the 164ft chimney. To help reduce 'down-time' on the economisers, they were fitted with mechanical scrapers each operated by its own small steam engine to keep them as clean as reasonably possible in their somewhat dirty duties and thus aid heat transfer, or at least delay the time at which diminution of heat transfer became insufferable.

The engine house was 183ft long by 60ft wide, a size which might seem somewhat extravagant until it is realised that the dynamos were driven

Right:
The main switchboard at the generating station as it was from 1893-95.

not by one of the new direct coupling designs of engine which were becoming available for electricity generation, but by conventional mill engines. These were supplied (as was all the rest of the steam equipment) by the famous mill-driving firm of Musgrave's of Bolton and were designed to deliver 400hp (indicated) at 100rpm. Like most heavy steam plant they were capable of sustaining an output well above this for short periods of need. They were of horizontal cross-compound configuration with cylinders of 15½in (HP) and 31in (LP). The stroke was 36in. Admission of steam at the normal working pressure of 120lbs psi was controlled by Corliss valve gear with the usual 'wrist plate' arrangement and a variable expansion governor.

Drive was by the conventional arrangement of multiple ropes, 19 in number and of 1¼in diameter working in grooves in the 3ft 2in wide periphery of the 14ft flywheel, which was also equipped with gear teeth for the barring engine. Engaging with these teeth, when required, were pinions on a shaft which ran the full length of the four main engines, driven by a single barring engine situated between Number 2 & 3. (The engines were numbered from the North) to carry out the vital function on turning an engine off the dead centre if it had chanced perversely to stop there when coming to rest.

Although mill machinery was generally very reliable if adequately maintained, a number of special features were incorporated to attempt to ensure that nothing would disrupt the service of trains. All pipework was prevented from causing trouble by leakage or stop valve failures by the simple expedient of duplicating everything, but more interesting was the condensing arrangement, where two entirely separate surface condensers, each capable of handling the exhaust steam of three main engines were so installed as to be completely interchangeable. Their air and circulating pumps were likewise interchangeable, each set driven by its own Ferguson-type non dead-centre vertical engine, with cylinders of 8½in (HP) and 14in (LP) and a stroke of 11in, at a normal speed of 80rpm. Lest belt and braces should both fail, there was also provision for allowing the main engines to exhaust direct to atmosphere, which would have terrible effects on the thermal efficiency, but would keep the wheels turning while repairs to the condensing equipment were effected.

Each main engine drove its own main dynamo at 420rpm, the rope drives being proportioned to achieve this measure of 'gearing up'. The dynamos by Elwell-Parker Ltd of Wolverhampton, were of the two-pole shunt-wound drum type, each producing 500Vdc at 500A. This represented 335ehp, some 16½% less than the rated output of the engines, to allow for losses in the ropes and bearings. Again thought had been given to reliability, and the dynamos were made of the double limb type, so that, with a magnetic circuit above and below the armature it was possible to have the poles cut through horizontally along the centre line with no ill effect. This allowed the removal of the upper half with the minimum of dismantling, and provision of a coupling in the armature shaft inboard of the driving end bearing meant that the armature itself could be removed without disturbing the rope drives. Massively built, (the complete dynamo weighed 21½ton, the armature alone 3ton) they were capable of standing considerable overload,

Above:
The main switchboard in 1895, as described in chapter 6.

and indeed would bear such an electrical overload as to be able to check the engines in the event of a permanent short circuit on the track.

Power from the dynamos passed to the main switchboard via an ammeter and a magnetic cut-out to common busbars, so that all, or any combination of the dynamos could work in parallel. The cut-out also served as the means of switching in or out its particular dynamo, which meant that all were kept in regular use and the less likely to stick when their services were urgently required to protect the generating plant against overload. This they were adjusted to do when a current of 1000A (double the normal load) was reached, and their protection was frequently invoked by the long-suffering system during the trial runs, when odd barrows, trolleys and other bits of equipment left lying around by the permanent way contractors caused frequent short circuits. (Incidentally, this led to the discovery that shorting the supply with any convenient hefty lump of iron made a very passable emergency stopping arrangement.) From the busbars, current passed to the main magnetic cut-out, which was set to break circuit at 3000-4000A, and thence to the track via four 37/13 Callender cables, which were lead sheathed and steel armoured, separate connections being made to up and down lines in each direction. No additional feeder cables were used in the original arrangement.

The contract for the whole of the electrical work had been won by the Electric Construction Corporation Ltd of Wolverhampton, and the work was designed and carried out under the supervision of Thomas Parker, who was the founder of that company, as well as being its General Manager and Engineer. In common with some other early electrical engineering contracts the terms included a provision for the contractor to show his confidence in his (often untried) skills by accepting some degree of liability for the initial success of operation, a liability which the Electric Construction Corporation satisfactorily discharged. The total cost of the generating installation was £36,000, a sum which in 1982 would not suffice for the construction and installation of one Lancashire boiler!

4. The Rolling Stock

Despite the fact that the world's first electric railway vehicle had been demonstrated as recently as 1879 there was no shortage of firms eager and apparently able to undertake the construction of the stock, but the successful tenderer was again the Electric Construction Corporation Ltd of Wolverhampton. They contracted to supply the whole of the rolling stock, which was to consist of 30 motor coaches, or 15 two-car trains. The actual carriage building was sub-contracted to the firm of Brown Marshall & Co. Ltd., perhaps better known by their later name of Metropolitan-Cammell, of Saltley, who delivered the bodies to the Wolverhampton works of the Electric Construction Corporation, where they were united with their bogies. The first was made available there, for inspection by the Directors of the LOR, on 11 January 1892, and it appears they were well pleased with what they saw. The vehicles were then sent on to Seaforth Sands where the electrical equipment was fitted to them at the carriage shed and works of the Railway.

The carriages were built of Burma Teak, with a length of 45ft, 8ft 6in wide and overall height above the rail of 11ft ⅝in seating 41 second class and 16 first class passengers. The small, single central buffers increased the overall length to 47ft 2in. These have sometimes been mistaken for a coupling, but in fact chain couplings, one either side of the buffer were employed. The bogies were mounted on 32ft centres and were of Fox's patent pressed steel type, with a wheelbase of 7ft and wheel diameter of 2ft 9in. To the leading axle was fitted the 60hp motor, while the three trailing axles were each equipped with brakes operated by the Westinghouse automatic compressed air system. The total weight of a coach was approximately 20ton, of which electrical equipment accounted for 6ton 7cwt, and the motor bogie for 5ton 7cwt; the motor alone, without wheels weighed 3ton.

The armatures were built directly onto the axles, and initially a drum type winding, four layers deep, was adopted to develop the necessary starting torque, and while this was quite satisfactory in tests and from an electrical point of view, it was viewed as highly suspect from a mechanical stance, with the result that a number of other arrangements was tried, of which the Eickmeyer system was adopted. This was described at the time as a winding

Left:
Motor composite No 2. *C. E. Box*

Above:
Front view of one of the trains after the number had been added. *C. E. Box*

Nº 1

SMOKING
THIRD
3
3

Far left:
LOR Train circuit breaker of 1892 which was mounted on the inside of the roof in the driver's cab.

Bottom left:
Close-up of bogie showing brake block, collector shoe etc. *C. E. Box*

Left:
Close-up of a controller for the electric stock. *C. E. Box*

Below:
Motor cars Nos 37, 18 and 41 in the sheds. *C. E. Box*

handrail of the structure airtight for the three-quarters of a mile or so which separated the trains from their air supply. The compressor at the south end was a slightly later addition, presumably to take account of increased route mileage, and each was driven by an electric motor with a gas engine provided as standby.

As originally built the coaches varied from the majority of those seen in photographs, and from the surviving example in Merseyside Museum, in not having a full-width driver's cab. Initially the driver was left to work in a compartment which could charitably be called pokey, 5ft long and only 3ft wide. The five windows across the front were, before the mounting of number panels and lights, allocated as two for the driver and three for the passengers, the oil head and rear lamps being fixed on an external bracket. The interior lighting for the passengers was provided

Top:
Bodybuilding at Seaforth Works. *C. E. Box*

Above:
***Lively Polly* with ice-cutter attached for cleaning the conductor rail.** *C. E. Box*

Above right:
***Polly* at work with engineering department open wagon.** *C. E. Box*

by 32 candlepower glow lamps, which were connected in series with the traction current.

Electric multiple units could not, of course, satisfy the needs of the LOR's maintenance team for hauling men and materials, especially if they were needed to rectify any sort of failure on the electrical side or in the vicinity of the conductor rails, and for this reason the Company owned one small steam locomotive, known as *Lively Polly*, though this appears to have been a term of endearment used by staff rather than an official name. *Polly* was built by Kitson's of Leeds in 1893, and was an 0-4-0T of diminutive proportions, 15ft 11in over her buffer beams and weighing only 10ton 2cwt in working order. Her 3ft dia wheels were on a 6ft wheelbase and she stood a mere 9ft 4in high.

She was reboilered more than once, but the original boiler was of 2ft 9in dia with 73 tubes of 1⅝in dia, which provided a heating surface of 136.5sq ft while the firebox had a heating surface of 23sq ft with a grate area of 6.4sq ft. The working pressure was 150lbs psi. Measured at 85% working pressure the two 8in bore by 12in stroke cylinders produced a tractive effort of 2,720lb. Her water consumption must have been very modest, for her well tank contained only 200gall.

Polly's normal train consisted of a 4-wheel semi-closed wagon and a 4-wheel tool van loaded with breakdown equipment, but she also served for inspections, hauling a first class trailer car and also occasionally faced heavy work in hauling new rails on 4-wheel carriage bogies. The bank from Seaforth and Litherland to Seaforth Sands with this latter load was her heaviest job. Small though she was, she gave good service from the opening of the railway until 1947, and North West enthusiasts might be interested to know that Kitson's had supplied three similar locomotives to the West Lancashire Railway in 1884, to run the Southport-Crossens services.

Maintenance facilities for the stock were provided at the old carriage shed, which was about 1000ft out of Seaforth Sands (new) Station towards Gladstone. Built over the top of the workshops, it was about 200ft long and 75ft wide, with five roads, each long enough to accommodate two two-car trains except for No. 3 road, which provided a well in the floor for lowering complete bogies to the workshops below, and hence could hold only one train. Trains undergoing overhaul or rebuilding stood at the end of one or other of the long roads. Such circumstances were scarcely ideal for body repair work, and were exacerbated by the fact that the shed was of such miserly height that an overhead crane was out of the question, and all lifting operations had to be undertaken by hand. Indeed a report existed to the effect that the shed as first built had doorways which were not high enough to allow a train to enter. Serious mechanical and electrical work took place below, and it was also at ground level that the compressor and storage tank for charging the trains' brake reservoirs were housed, while above, on a mezzanine some 6ft high, stood the offices of the Engineer and his assistant, commanding a fine view over the shed and the coachbuilders' workshop.

5. Opening the Line

The weather in Liverpool was not pleasant on 7 January 1893, but the Directors of the Company had other matters on their mind, for at 1.30pm they rode on the first train to run on the line. A party of guests, including C. A. Rowlandson, the Manager of the Mersey Railway; Thomas Parker, Chief Engineer and General Manager of the Electric Construction Corporation; J. H. Woodward and D. Meldrum, together with the engineers for the line and a group of pressmen were received by the Chairman, Sir W. B. Forwood, and boarded the train at Pier Head. The train then ran to each terminus and returned for the distinguished party to inspect the generating station. This was followed by the obligatory dinner at the Adelphi Hotel, where Mr Parker took the chair.

In February the preliminaries for the official opening of the line began (which was perhaps curious as the Board of Trade inspection had not yet been made) with the arrival of the Prime Minister, Lord Salisbury, at *Ramleh*, the Blundellsands residence of Sir William Forwood. A large house party was assembled to greet him, among its number some eminent figures from the world of science and engineering, including Lord Kelvin. The occasion was notable from a scientific point of view in that the National Telephone Company had arranged a display of its technical expertise which enabled guests to listen to parts of live performances in theatres at London and Manchester, while as a special tour de force they had made the first ever telephone connection to the House of Commons, by means of which Lord Salisbury was able to hear part of the progress of a debate.

The following morning Lord Salisbury drove down to the generating station, escorted by mounted police, where he was formally

Below:
The railway at Pier Head soon after the opening, in 1893. One of the competing horse-buses can be seen behind the structure.

Above:

An early view of Pier Head, Liverpool, soon after the opening of the railway. Note the square rigged vessel and ships in the river and the absence of electric trams.

welcomed by Sir William, who in doing so, made a speech in which he explained how the opening of the Liverpool and Manchester Railway had been the decisive step in the universal adoption of the steam locomotive for rail haulage, and expressed the not unreasonable suggestion that some parallel might be drawn. The railway they were there to open might only be a little over five miles long, but it was the first in this country on an iron viaduct, the first to be served over a distance of five miles by a generating system, and the first to be protected by electric automatic signalling. It might well be as important a pioneer as its august predecessor, and the precedent for electric railways in all our great cities.

His Lordship responded, and then pressed the button concealed in the base of a large silver inkstand which was the means of setting the main engines in motion. This had the not necessarily unfortunate effect that the later and lesser orators were not easily heard above the sounds of the machinery. After the speeches the inkstand was detached from the mechanism it had concealed, and presented to Lord Salisbury as a gift to mark the occasion. It was not only a handsome gift, but an instructive one also, being bordered with representations of ships' cables, indicative of Liverpool's calling as a great port, a chasing depicting the power and swiftness of electricity, and finally an ingenious model of a part of the Overhead Railway featuring the bow girder bridge opposite St. Nicholas' Church. There followed a trip up the line for the assembled VIPs in a specially decorated train before Lord Salisbury was entertained by the Lord Mayor.

The railway was inspected on behalf of the Board of Trade by Major-General Hutchinson RE, CB, Major Cardew RE and Major York RE over a period of four days during which every one of the spans, which numbered over 500, had to be carefully examined. The test load for the ordinary part of the structure was four trains, each loaded with weights to equal a full complement of passengers. In order to simulate the worst combination of loads it was stipulated that the trains should be coupled with their motor

THE LIVERPOOL
OVERHEAD
RAILWAY
A SPLENDID VIEW OF
THE DOCKS
& RIVER.
FIRST & FASTEST
ELECTRIC
(OVERHEAD) RAILWAY
IN THE WORLD.
RAPID AND FREQUENT SERVICE
OF SALOON CARS AT
CHEAP FARES
Affording Magnificent Panoramic View
OF THE LIVERPOOL DOCKS
6½ miles in extent
AND THE RIVER MERSEY.
31, JAMES ST LIVERPOOL
S.B. COTTRELL M.Inst.C.E.
ENGINEER & GENERAL MANAGER
THE LIVERPOOL PRINTING & STATIONERY CO LIMITED

Left:
An LOR poster in the 1890s advertising the splendid views of the docks. Note the passengers looking out of the three left hand front windows of the train. *George Cohen 600 Group*

Above:
The Langton lift bridge prior to the opening of the line. Note the absence of any conductor rail.

Far left:
Driver's view at the bottom of the 'Switchback' under the high level coal bridge. *C. E. Box*

Left and bottom left:
Driver's view of the Brunswick bridge being lifted. *C. E. Box*

Below:
View from the end of the platform at Seaforth Sands old station.

BOOK CHEAP EXCURSION TICKETS
EGREMONT NEW BRIGHTON TOWER EASTHAM
BLINKERS
BLINKERS

lin417 lin146

Above left and above:
Two views of the exterior of Seaforth Sands station c1922. The bridge across Fort Road connected the old and new stations. Note a tram for Great Crosby in a siding clear of the main road. The square brick building seen above the new station roof (left hand building) housed the electric passenger lift.

Left:
Drivers view of the line. Note the centre 'third' rail, colour light signal and automatic train stop. *Ian Allan Library*

Bottom:
'See the ships' the advertisements said . . . . .

Below:
Crowds waiting for a train at Huskisson Dock station. *C. E. Box*

Right:
Advertisements on huts near Blundell Sands.

bogies together instead of at the ends of the train as was the intended practice. This load amounted to about 13cwt per linear foot on each line of the railway, and it was discovered that the deflection on 40ft span was ⅛in, while on the longest span (of 75ft) it was ½in. The part of the structure which appears to have worried the inspectors was the double-deck movable bridge at Stanley Dock, for there they required that same load on the upper deck together with four of the heaviest of the Lancashire & Yorkshire Railway's tank locomotives (the Dock Board at this time having no locomotives of its own) on the lower deck. These weighed together about 30cwt per linear foot per rail in addition to the 13cwt per foot above, but the bridge sustained the weight with a deflection at the centre of only ⅜in. These, together with all the other tests, proved satisfactory.

The Company had, as yet, little knowledge of the electrical loads which would be imposed by trains under particular circumstances, for the pioneering nature of the undertaking ensured that there was no great corpus of precedent and experience on which to draw. It was necessary, therefore, to operate some trial trains, and one of these ran on 5 March. A test train was assembled and loaded with iron weights to simulate a full load of passengers; it started from Herculaneum and travelled to Alexandra. The distance was approximately 5⅛ miles (or 9030.4 yards to be exact), and the total time taken was 24min 57sec, an average speed of 12.3mph. If the time stopped, which amounted to 4min 35sec, was deducted this left an actual running average of 15mph. The average current while running was 82.7A corresponding to 54.4ehp. Taken over the whole trip, including standing and coasting, the averages were respectively 67.3A and 44.4ehp, with an average emf over the trip of 485.2V.

To find the effect of speed on power requirement a second trip was taken at a slightly brisker pace, the train having returned to Herculaneum 'off the record'. The total time was reduced to 23min 47sec, of which current was on the cars for 15min 18sec and it was actually at a stand for 4min 40sec. This produced an overall average speed of 13mph, a running average of 16.1mph. This greater exertion demanded an average current while running of 90.8A (73A overall) corresponding to 57.1ehp running, 44.4 overall, and caused the emf to fall to 484V. Current consumption under actual running conditions could be determined from the daily log sheet at the generating station, but to evaluate the data thus obtained it was necessary to have recorded results from the footplate.

The following day, the railway began, without further ceremony, to operate its normal service to the public, starting at 5.00am with trains every ten minutes until 8.00am, whence the service was of five minutes until 7.00pm. The frequency then reverted to ten minutes until close-down at 9.00pm. Until the introduction of complications of through bookings to other destinations the fare structure was simple in the extreme: any journey on the whole or any part of the line cost 2d second class, 3d first class with the single variation that a workman's return was available before 8.00am for 3d. Whilst this was a substantial increase on the 1d fare on the horse bus, the immense time saving (the bus typically took 1¼ hours from Herculaneum to Alexandra) proved quite adequate incentive to passengers, with the result that within the first complete half-year of working (that ended 31 December 1893) the railway carried almost as many passengers in those six months as the buses carried in a year. In handling this very substantial traffic the simplicity of checking passengers through the turnstiles, and of ticket issue must have been a very real assistance, with only three types of ticket in use.

Of the 15 two-car trains the railway owned, eight were needed for the morning ten-minute service, twelve for the five-minute service, and six, reducing to four, for the evening ten-minute service.

6. Extending the line

As originally envisaged, the line of the railway suffered from one serious disadvantage. The daytime traffic which could be anticipated was enormous, and there would doubtless be some evening demand from sailors on shore leave in search of the proverbial good time, but it did not tap any major residential areas. To keep fares up as far around the clock as possible it was plainly desirable to broaden the commuter appeal, and this, as it happened could be done fairly simply, by adding a short extension at each end of the line. This became apparent to the Board at an early stage, and before the original line had been completed powers had been obtained for the construction of the extensions.

At the North end, the line already extended beyond the passenger terminus at Alexandra, towards the Old carriage shed, so that only 342 yards of new double track were necessary to take the terminus on another three-quarters of a mile to the new station of Seaforth Sands, which not only approached more desirable commuter territory, but was also a step towards a connection with the Lancashire & Yorkshire Railway at Seaforth & Litherland. The short new portion was built on precisely similar principles to the rest of the structure, and with the same engineering team of Sir Douglas Fox, J. H. Greathead and S. B. Cottrell. There were no particular engineering problems except for the need for another bowstring bridge to cross the roadway which is now the main entrance to Gladstone Dock. The Contractors were Holmes and King of Liverpool, with Pearson & Knowles of Warrington and the Phoenix Foundry Co. of Derby as sub-contractors. The extra section was duly inspected by Major-General Hutchinson and Major Cardew, approved, and opened for traffic on 30 April 1894.

A further short extension at the North was made in 1905 which was of possibly greater consequence in terms of potential new commuter traffic, this being the short stretch up to Seaforth & Litherland. A new station was built at Seaforth Sands virtually alongside the old one, whence the track swung away to the east, crossing Crosby Road South to the new junction. It might seem nowadays that a mere facility for passengers to change trains would have sufficed, but in these heady days of early electric traction through running was immediately envisaged, and the LOR began to convert its supply rails from the original channel section laid in the 4ft to flat bottomed rails laid in the 6ft, in order that their stock could run over the Lancashire & Yorkshire's rails, while the L&YR built some special lightweight stock in order to be able to run through to Dingle over the elevated structure. The line was opened to traffic on 2 July 1905. Although the through L&YR trains, after having been increased from single coach to two and sometimes three-coach units running every hour, had ceased in 1913, the outside conductors, which were of 70lb/yd rail laid with their centres 19¼in from gauge, as per L&YR, remained. The old channel section rails remained as a return in addition to the running rails, a function they continued to discharge until their removal in 1922. Standardisation did not reach to the carriage sidings however, for the old channel section conductors remained in use both at Herculaneum and on the roads leading into the new carriage sheds at Seaforth until the closure of the railway. The old station at Seaforth Sands continued in use alongside the old until 1925, when it was closed and demolished.

The cooperation with the L&YR was taken a stage further in 1906, with another short extension to the north, this time taking the form of a double line junction at Rimrose Road with the line to Aintree. The principal purpose of this junction was to provide a service to Aintree racecourse on just two days a year, Grand National Day and Jump Sunday. In those days of fewer amusements, all of local High Society, together with many thousands whose society was less elevated made the annual pilgrimages to Aintree, and transport facilities were, to put it mildly, stretched. On those days through services between Dingle and Aintree were run using both LOR stock and L&YR lightweight stock. These latter trains were also used for a through service to Alexandra Dock until about 1922.

The Southern Extension commenced at a new junction just to the north of Herculaneum Station, where a new station was built, leaving the old

Above:
View over Herculaneum Dock showing the old station on the left, later used as a carriage shed when the line was extended to Dingle over the longest bridge on the LOR system. *C. E. Box*

Below:
The CLC sheds at Brunswick showing the footbridge from Grafton Street to the new Herculaneum station. *C. E. Box*

Above:
The new station at Herculaneum; the old station can just be seen in the background. *C. E. Box*

Below:
The approach to Dingle tunnel. *C. E. Box*

Above right:
The new station at Seaforth Sands. *C. E. Box*

one at the end of a short spur to serve as a carriage shed. The main line curved to the South East, over about 250yds of overhead viaduct of the normal pattern towards a tunnel portal in the rock face to the landward side of the dock. In between lay the considerable expanse of the Cheshire Lines Railway's goods yard, which extended from their station at Brunswick Dock, and to clear this obstacle it was necessary to build the longest bridge on the line. This bridge was of lattice girder type, with parallel booms, the main girders being respectively 220ft and 225ft long: the complete bridge weighed some 212ton and had a clear span of 200ft.

Dingle Tunnel was arched throughout and for the first 605yds was 25ft 6in wide and 19ft high. It was by no means an easy undertaking, for the red sandstone in which it was cut was a particularly treacherous material with heavy backs and wet clay beds often being encountered, making heavy timbering necessary during excavation. Many of the crown bars had to be built in, and the entire length had to be lined with brindle bricks. Because it was only a short tunnel it was felt unnecessary to employ any of the new types of tunnelling machinery available, and it was cut by the traditional methods of sinking shafts at intervals and joining them up by manual labour backed up with simple black powder. This process was not aided by the fact that the ground above was almost entirely built upon, which made the choice of sites for shafts very circumscribed. Five shafts were sunk, each of them 10ft sq, and headings of 11ft or 12ft driven in each direction from them. Alignment was good, and the greatest error discovered in either plane at a breakthrough was a mere ¾in. This alone, however, was no cause for self-congratulation, for the engineers and contractors faced worse problems than merely getting the hole in the right place. About 170ft into the tunnel it had to pass over another of the CLC lines which also burrowed through towards Dingle, at a slightly lower level than that needed for the LOR. It was the slightness in the difference of level which caused the problem: the crossing, which was at an agle of 28°, could be made only with a clearance of a mere 2ft 9in between the LOR rails and the top of the arch of the CLC tunnel. Obviously the LOR company had only been able to get powers to build the tunnel at the expense of an undertaking that they would not impose any additional load upon the arch of the existing CLC tunnel, so that the engineers had to adopt a segmental arch to carry their track bed over the lower tunnel with an air gap of 6in between the bottom of the former and the top of the latter. To make the task more difficult still, the CLC held powers to build another tunnel to the east of the one then in use,

LANCASHIRE & YORKSHIRE RAILWAY
AND
LIVERPOOL OVERHEAD RAILWAY.
CHURCHTOWN
CROSSENS
TO PRESTON
HESKETH PARK
St LUKES
SOUTHPORT
THROUGH CONNECTION
AND
THROUGH BOOKINGS
TO AND FROM ALL STATIONS
BETWEEN SEAFORTH, SOUTHPORT & CROSSENS. (INCLUSIVE)
ON THE
SOUTHPORT BRANCH
OF THE
LANCASHIRE & YORKSHIRE
RAILWAY
AND ALL
STATIONS ON THE
LIVERPOOL
OVERHEAD
RAILWAY.
TO PRESTON
BIRKDALE
AINSDALE
FRESHFIELD
FORMBY GOLF LINKS
FORMBY
ALTCAR
ALTCAR RIFLE RANGE
HIGHTOWN
WEST LANCASHIRE GOLF LINKS
AINTREE
HALL ROAD
CAPTAINS LANE
BLUNDELLSANDS AND CROSBY
WATERLOO
LINACRE ROAD
SEAFORTH AND LITHERLAND
SEAFORTH SANDS
MARSH LANE AND STRAND ROAD
BOOTLE
BOOTLE
BANKHALL
ALEXANDRA
SANDHILLS
LANGTON
LIVERPOOL EXCHANGE STATION L&Y RAILWAY
BROCKLEBANK
CANADA
HUSKISSON
NELSON
CLARENCE
PRINCE'S
LIVERPOOL
PIERHEAD
JAMES ST
CUSTOM HOUSE
WAPPING
BRUNSWICK
TOXTETH
DINGLE
HERCULANEUM
L&Y. RY THUS
LIV. OVERD RY THUS
J.A.F. ASPINALL, GENERAL MANAGER.
LANCASHIRE & YORKSHIRE RAILWAY,
HUNTS BANK, MANCHESTER.
E. J. NEACHELL, GENERAL MANAGER.
LIVERPOOL OVERHEAD RAILWAY.
31, JAMES STREET, LIVERPOOL.
THE LIVERPOOL PRINTING & STATIONERY Co LIMITED

Left:
Poster issued c1910 drawing attention to the through connections. *George Cohen 600 Group*

and these powers too had been protected, so that the LOR decided the simplest course was to build a short stretch of this proposed new tunnel under their own and support their tunnel on its arch. Undertaken entirely by manual labour it proved to be a most difficult and expensive operation, but at least it guaranteed that services would not be disrupted in the future. After overcoming these problems the encountering of a 5ft by 3ft sewer a little further on must not have seemed too serious, but it was necessary to change the form of the tunnel arch from semi-circular to segmental for a short way, which just allowed space for the sewer to be underpinned.

Dingle Station had an island platform situated in a widened section of tunnel which began 605yds from the entrance, the width increasing to 52ft and the height to 24ft 6in for a length of 163yds, beyond which lay a further 41yds of tunnel of normal section, ending with a dead wall, which accommodated two sidings and a single crossover. The station itself could, at the time of opening, boast the largest tunnel arch in Britain, a somewhat paradoxical superlative for an overhead railway. At the East end of the platform a flight of steps led to an overbridge, whence the passenger ascended an inclined subway just over 50yds long into the booking hall. The exit (and entrance) opened onto Park Road, just by the end of Kedleston Street, on a site now occupied by a car showroom.

For the first few years of operation, the trains were equipped with a belt and braces lighting system, to minimise the risk of a train which became stranded also being blacked out. This was operated by a pick-up on the roof of the carriages, which collected current from an overhead copper conductor mounted in the tunnel, the current for which was provided by accumulators. The station itself was lit by electricity from the outset, originally by arc lights operated at 110V from the traction supply via a rotary transformer. A standby system of battery lighting was provided in case of a short circuit on the track causing total lighting failure.

The construction of the southern extension was undertaken by the same team of engineers as was the rest of the line. The contractor for the elevated portion was again Pearson & Knowles, of Warrington, while the tunnel portion was built by H. M. Nowell and C. Braddock. Having been inspected and passed fit, the extension was opened to traffic on 21 December 1896. The railway had now reached its full extent of 567 spans, with a total weight of structure of some 23,000ton and a total length of 7 miles and 160 yards.

Power

The opening of the extensions to north and south implied a growth in traffic, to meet which eight new motor coaches had been ordered, and these would, of course, increase the demands upon the generating station. To meet this extra demand the output of the power station was increased by no less than 50%, from 1,200ehp to 1,800ehp by the addition of further main engines and dynamos. The new engines were numbered 5 & 6, and were built by another eminent mill machinery constructor, namely Hick, Hargreaves of Bolton. The new engines, like the original sets by Musgrave, were built according to mill practice, with multiple rope drives from the flywheel rim, and were designed for an output of 400ihp each. The configuration was again horizontal cross compound, with cylinder dimensions of 15½in (hp) and 31in (lp) by 36in stroke. Steam admission was by Corliss trip gear with direct-acting variable expansion governor. Service speed was 100rpm, and the 14ft dia flywheel had a face of 3ft 2in grooved for 19 ropes of 1¼in dia. Although the engines were basically conventional they did embody two unusual features, one of which was a new type governor which was claimed to produce as much power in action as previous types while reducing inertia and thus increasing sensitivity of response to varying loads. Novelty did not extend, however, to driving the governors by anything more positive than rope, an unfortunately common practice. (Since a governor cannot fail safe if it stops rotating, or the engine would never start, a failure of the governor drive means an almost inevitable 'runaway'.)

The other innovation was the replacement of the usual one-piece cylinder and valve chest casting with a composite block built up of four different, and comparatively simple, castings. These were: the working cylinder; the jacket; two end castings containing the valve chambers. Such an arrangement had a number of advantages, including the enhanced ease and cheapness of repair in the event of wear or failure and the

View of the new works under construction. The tramway maintenance vehicle is seen parked at the front near one of the trams.
E. Wood & Co

ability to choose the optimum material for each of a number of different functions instead of the compromise which was usually necessary. The only disadvantage was a possible slight loss of rigidity, but the casting of a single block was such a complicated affair that locked-in stresses sometimes caused them to break quite unaided, and on balance the new design had to be a great improvement.

Steam was exhausted to an additional condenser, which was 3ft 8½in long by 7ft 8in long between tube plates, divided into three clusters of ¾in brass tubes containing 337, 343 and 339 tubes respectively, a total cooling surface of 1,500sq ft.

The new main dynamos were by Thomas Parker & Co. Ltd of Wolverhampton, and produced an output of 250kW (500A at 500V) at a speed of 420rpm. The armatures had been designed to have identical external dimensions with those of the old dynamos, in order that they should be interchangeable. They were built on shafts 5in dia, with three bearings, one at the commutator end and one either side of the drive pulley. These bearings were 1ft 5in long, and the one at the commutator end was of spherical form. Complete, the armature assembly weighed 3ton 2cwt. The magnets were of a special magnetic steel, of the highest permeability available, and were arranged with patented hinged pole pieces which allowed access to the armatures for inspection, cleaning or lifting without the need to unset the bearings; a drive coupling between pulley and armature meant that the drive also could be left undisturbed. The total weight of the dynamos was 24½ tons (each).

There had been some variation in emf noticeable on the line, which would likely be increased by the increased length and load, so at the same time that the new plant was put in, feeder cables were installed for the first time. These were three in number, all on the positive pole, connecting each from the main busbar to, respectively, up and down conductor rails at James Street, up conductor at Brunswick and Toxteth, and down conductor at Brunswick and Toxteth.

A new main switchboard was also installed by Thomas Parker & Co, which consisted of six slate panels, corresponding each to its own dynamo. The equipment mounted on them was identical throughout and consisted of the following: 1. A patent double-pole automatic cut-out. These could be closed and opened by hand, and thus doubled in function as main switches for the dynamos. Lest a short circuit on the line should cause one to open with excessive load and injure the operator through the arc thus created, each was equipped with a plate glass protector. The magnets were compound wound so that they would also break immediately in the case of current reversal. 2. A single-pole throw-over (knife) switch for connecting the dynamo circuit beyond the automatic cut-out to the busbar feeding the line at the nearest point to the generating station or to a feeder cable to a distant point on the line in order to equalise the emf. 3. A 33-way sliding regulating switch to vary the resistance in the dynamo shunt circuit, in order to maintain the emf of each dynamo constant. 4. A pair of double-pole plugs for connecting a voltmeter to the dynamo before paralleling. 5. A Weston 0-600 amp moving coil ammeter, showing the current passing from the dynamo to the line.

The slate panels were mounted up on an iron frame, handsomely finished with carved teak of massive proportions, and above them were the clock and four Weston 0-600V meters, mounted in panelled framework. The voltmeters were respectively connected across the main busbars, for connection at will to any dynamo by means of plugs, as mentioned above, for connection across the brushes of the dynamo running on the feeder circuit, and as a pilot meter connected to the distant point of a feeder which was coupled. In the somewhat alarming manner of installations of the period, the back of the board was not festooned with insulated cable, but bristled with substantial bronze bars, supported on pillars. Access for testing and maintenance was superb, but behind the board was plainly no place for the uninitiated!

Like its equally diminutive neighbour, the

Right:
The feeder cables at Brunswick Dock station.
C. E. Box

Below right:
LOR stock at Gateacre in July 1952! A 'fake' photograph looking North and produced to give an impression of the proposed 'Belt Route'. The LOR train has been skilfully superimposed on an existing scene, but someone forgot to add a conductor rail!

Mersey Railway, the Overhead saw connections with outside railways as being potentially very beneficial, and in 1903 powers were obtained to build a further short extension. At the south end a short stretch of new railway would run from Herculaneum to join the Cheshire Lines' route at St. Michael's Station, and these, taken in conjunction with powers obtained the following year to join Seaforth Sands with Cheshire Lines at Sefton Station would have made the Overhead into one leg of a circular route around Liverpool. It would follow the present Merseyrail route as far as Hunts Cross and then take the now defunct CLC route via Gateacre and West Derby to Sefton, where it would meet the new Seaforth and Sefton Junction railway. Sadly, this was a time when the Overhead had been making heavy investments elsewhere and when revenue was declining slightly due to the onslaught of the Corporation Tramways, so that nothing materialised before the First World War began, and the uncertainties of the twenties, together with losses of ocean liner passenger traffic to Southampton, ensured that nothing was built. Even a cut price version of the scheme, which used the North Mersey Branch (Lancashire & Yorkshire Railway) with a half mile spur to join CLC at Aintree and a shorter southern extension from Dingle to St. Michael's to achieve much the same objectives, came to nothing. In the light of hindsight it appears extraordinary that such a cheap and obviously sound scheme should fail, but sadly this is the last we hear of what was then known as the 'Belt Route'.

7. The LOR Tramway

It was in 1897, while Liverpool's first electric tram service was under construction, that some pressure arose in the urban districts of Great Crosby and Waterloo-with-Seaforth for the introduction of an electric tramway to improve upon the service offered by the horse buses which travelled the main route out of Liverpool to Crosby. The matter was discussed at some length by the respective district councils, who eventually contented themselves with a policy statement to the effect that a tramway should indeed be constructed through their area, but declining to do anything about executing this policy. Their intention, very plainly, was that some other public body, or a private firm, should build and operate the tramway. The horsebus service was actually operated by the Corporation of Liverpool in 1897, but it was the Overhead Railway Company which made an offer to provide all the electrical equipment and stock, and to operate the tramway. Late in 1898 this offer was considered by the councils and accepted, the proposal being then put before Parliament and duly authorised the following year.

The line began at the LOR terminus at Seaforth Sands, and proceeded a distance of 2mile 40chains to Victoria Road, Great Crosby. Experimental runs were made on 13 June 1900, and the service officially commenced over the first mile of the route, to the point known as 'The Five Lamps', where the tramway crossed over the L&YR line to Southport. Trial runs on the section beyond were not very successful: poor alignment of the track caused a number of derailments, but by the beginning of October the defects had been rectified and the line opened throughout, when the horse bus service was withdrawn.

The line was single track throughout, with 14 passing places. At Seaforth Sands there was originally a single track in the middle of Crosby Road South, with a curved siding extending under the old station, and a line which ran about 150yds to the tram depot, which was located under the structure of the railway. Two roads ran the full length of the depot, each with an inspection pit extending almost to the far end. When the new station was built in 1905 a second curved siding was built to approach it, which had the desirable side effect that no longer might a waiting car obstruct the main road.

On leaving Seaforth Sands there was a slight rising gradient as far as Church Road, whence the next mile was almost entirely straight and level, and the only difficulty was that for about 200yds after South Road the main road was very narrow, widening out again before it reached the Crosby boundary at College Road. The line continued on a gentle curve, rising slightly from College Road to Myers Road West, falling to Endbutt Lane, levelling to Crosby Village and finally falling slightly again to the terminus. In all, it was a fairly well-laid out route, with no severe curves or gradients to cause problems.

By the time that the tramway was under construction the generating station was already beginning to feel the strain, with five out of six engines often required: this left no spare capacity when one engine was down for maintenance. There was therefore no doubt that the opening of the tramway would require further additions to the generating plant, even before the introduction of the anticipated accelerated service on the railway. The capacity of the boilerhouse was also fully utilised, since the additional engines of 1896 had not been paralleled by extra boilers.

One new Lancashire boiler was supplied by Musgrave's of Bolton. Although it was of the same length (30ft) as the original boilers, it was 1ft larger in diameter, at 9ft, and was equipped with a superheater. The working pressure (120lbs psi) was the same, as was the arrangement of Vickers mechanical stokers. The new engine, numbered 7, was entirely different from those previously installed, for it was a vertical triple tandem compound. Built by Browett, Lindley & Co. of Patricroft, it was a high speed fully enclosed engine, with pressure lubrication, of the type developed by and normally associated with, Belliss & Morcom. The builder's number was 1345, and the engine had bores of 17in hp and 30in lp with a stroke of 15in: its designed output was of 1,500bhp at 230rpm. The only space which was available to house it was at the south end of the engine house, where the roof was

Above:
One of the early open-top cars at Five lamps, Waterloo soon after the commencement of the service.

lower than elsewhere, so that the engine had to be sited in a pit to accommodate its height (about 12ft) while allowing headroom for maintenance work.

The engine was direct-coupled to the DC multipolar generator by British Schuckert of London which, at the service speed of 230rpm gave an output of 1,650A at 500V, 825kW. This generator was marked G7, but by 1909 it had been replaced by a 12-pole shunt wound generator by Dick, Kerr which had an output of 1,700A at 500V, 850kW. One additional condenser was also installed, to maintain the ability to leave one spare for cleaning or repair.

It appears on paper that this engine should have been more efficient than the comparatively lumbering mill-style engines of the previous installations, but such was not the case. With its short stroke, and lp:hp ratio of noticeably less than 1:2 its expansive ratio was lower and this lower ratio was naturally manifested in a marked hunger for steam as compared with the horizontals. It was, of course, massively more powerful for its bulk and weight, but such gains had to be paid for in coal, and although it was used regularly to begin with, it was eventually relegated to use in emergency and on Sundays, when it could meet the whole power requirement for the line on its own.

In order to reduce transmission losses on the tramway supply the voltage was increased by two rotary transformers, each fed from the 500V busbars and having an output of 80-150A at 1,100 to 1,150V. These, like the new generator, were supplied by British Schuckert, and were controlled by their own separate switchboard, with oil-immersed starters for the motors. At the other end of the cables was the tramway substation, which was under the railway at Seaforth Sands, adjacent to the tram shed. Here stood the corresponding pair of British Schuckert rotary transformers to transform the transmission voltage of 1,100 to 1,150 down to the traction voltage of 500 to 550. The transformers were not normally required in service together, and they were controlled from a magnificent marble board mounting the switchgear and highly polished instruments. Occasionally the load was so heavy as to require the use of both, and one such instance is clearly remembered by the author when, in 1914, thousands of soldiers were carried down from Great Crosby to Seaforth Sands to join the railway. Every tram was loaded

G! CROSBY. WATERLOO. SEAFORTH
7

Left:
The LOR Tram shed at Seaforth in 1924, showing the tower wagon in the left hand corner. This would connect behind a service tram and be towed to where it was required. The second door on right led to the Tramway sub-station.

Below left:
Car No 7 in its original condition.

to its absolute maximum, a sight which would never be forgotten by anyone who witnessed it.

The fourteen passing loops mentioned were situated at Henley Street, Church Road, Latham Avenue, Durham Road, Kinross Road, Great George's Road (The Five Lamps), South Road, St. John's Road, Marldon Avenue, Myers Road West, Endbutt Lane, Coronation Road and the terminus. A few weeks after the opening an additional loop was constructed at Little Crosby Road, but it was soon found that some of the loops were superfluous. By 1906 the loops at Henley Street, Myers Road West, Little Crosby and the terminus had been removed, while those at Latham Avenue, Durham Road and Kinross Road had been replaced by two new ones at Claremont Road and Cambridge Road, making a total of nine loops which remained unchanged until closure.

A slight digression is possibly called for to explain the meaning of the name 'The Five Lamps', which was not only a noted local landmark, but also the scene of a number of views of the tramway shown on commercial postcards. At the junction of Crosby Road with Great George's Road a small island stands in the middle of the intersection. Upon it stood a horse trough, and an unusual lamp standard, with five separate lamps, one large and four smaller. These were originally of conventional design, but soon after the opening of the tramway they were replaced by five highly ornate lamps of a cylindrical design favoured by the Waterloo-with-Seaforth UDC upon a new standard. The junction is still known locally as 'Five Lamps'.

Throughout its route the tramway was served with side bracket traction standards to carry its wires, their arms varying in length according to the width of the road. The two wires were invariably off centre and initially suspended at the same level. This made it necessary to fit the trolley poles with a curious bent extension in order to ensure that the outer wire was not contacted when running on the inner. Later the outer wires were suspended some 3in lower than the inner, which allowed the removal of the extensions. The ends of the trolley poles were considerably curved to prevent accidental contact with the inner wires.

Maintenance of the overhead equipment was effected by means of a tower wagon built as a horse-drawn road vehicle, with conventional metal tyred wheels. In practice it was rarely if ever used as such, being attached to the back of a tram and hauled as a trailer, a noisy procedure on the setts along the route.

The standards were mostly on the landward side of the track, the exceptions being the stretch between Myers Road West and Crosby Village and two individual examples which supported a pull-off, one at Church Road, Seaforth and the other in Crosby Village. These standards, together with the terminal one at Crosby and a couple at Seaforth Sands were of stouter dimensions than the normal design. All, however, were alike in having an ornamental base of the type used both by London United Tramways and the Bristol Tramways & Carriage Co. The finials were of two patterns: those in Waterloo-with-Seaforth and some of those in Crosby were of the orthodox ball and spike variety, while the remainder of those in Crosby were rather more ornate. A similar variation was to be found in the street lamps which were attached to the traction standards on a rental basis, the LOR receiving 1s 0d (5p) per pole per year for its pains.

In the later years of operation, an automatic trolley reverser was installed at Seaforth Sands, consisting of a wire joining the main line to the depot line, and a similar arrangement was adopted at Great Crosby about 1918, the last 30 or 40yds of track being served only by a single wire.

The original rolling stock consisted of 12 Preston-built cars of three types. Nos. 1-8 were uncanopied open-top cars similar to some already sold to Liverpool and other systems. They were 16ft long over the body with three side windows and with a 90° turn direct staircase. Their distinctive feature was a very high side rail on the upper deck, designed to prevent any possibility of passengers being struck by the traction pole of another tram at the passing loops. The empty weight of these cars was 8½ton, and their capacity was 22 passengers below and 28 above.

LIVERPOOL OVERHEAD RAILWAY

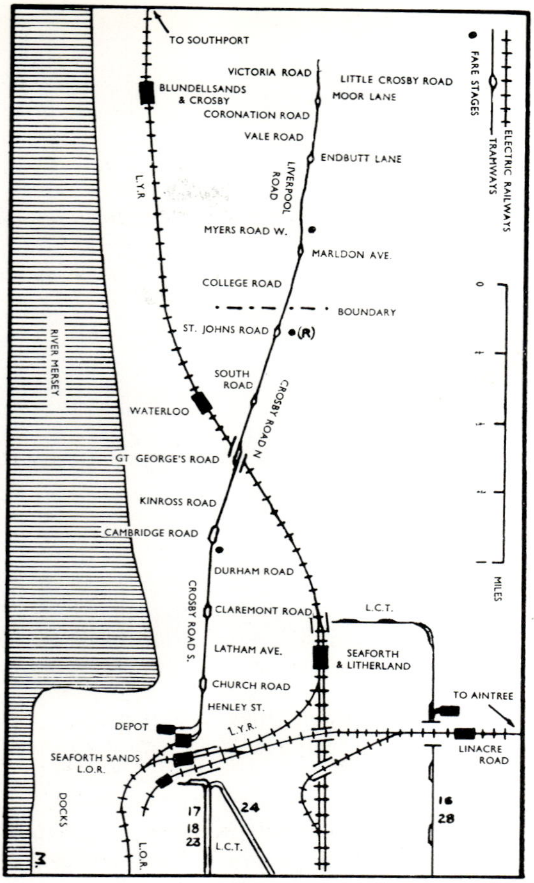

Left:

One of the original batch of trams. Note the high guard rails on the top deck, and the lettering and lining.

Above:
Car No 10 passing St. John's Road on the Crosby Road at Waterloo c1913. *S. S. Cushing*

Of the remainder, Nos 9 and 10 were single deckers, with full canopies and open sides. Known as 'summer cars' they were fitted with eight fixed benches and were capable of carrying 32-40 passengers, though the accommodation of five passengers per bench is said to have required that they be friendly, emaciated or preferably both! Nos 11 and 12 were double deckers, but of a later design than Nos 1-8, with canopied ends and reversed stairs. Like the earlier design, they had high side rails on the upper deck, though of a more elaborate type. A minor, but very obvious, difference was that the headlamp was moved down from the end of the upper deck to a position about halfway up the dash panel. These two cars were part of the original order, and presumably the reason for their differing from Nos 1-8 was the new design which appeared between order and delivery, with the Company being given the option of having two of the new type. Within a year two additional cars were ordered: Nos 13 and 14 were identical to Nos 11 and 12, in 1903 two further cars of the same type were obtained.

All these cars had the same truck underneath, by Brill, with a 6ft wheelbase and equipped with two 25hp motors, but the later type of body was both larger and heavier with a seating capacity of 22 below and 36 above and an empty weight of 9ton.

Body finish, as usual in the tram trade, was of a high standard. The panels were in green and cream, with elaborate lining out, and the name "Liverpool Overhead Railway Co." lettered out boldly along nearly the full length of the body, in deep shaded block style (though with an occasional Egyptian serif). The Company crest was prominently displayed on the waist panel. Destination boards being unnecessary, the signwriter had also to indicate the route "Seaforth-Waterloo-Great Crosby" on the sides of the upper deck. In the case of the open cars the lettering was in gold on a black background, while the covered-top cars had black deep-shaded lettering, with initial letters in red.

Over the years various alterations were made to the cars, the first significant one being the ordering of two completely new bodies from Dick, Kerr in 1912 which were presumably to be fitted to two of the trucks from cars of the first batch, probably Nos 5 and 7. These new bodies were similar to those of Nos 11-16 apart from having 180° direct staircases, and Nos 11-16 were gradually altered to the new arrangement. About 1914 the two single-deck cars were withdrawn from service, though No 10 remained

Above:
Another view of the Crosby Road and Five Lamps.

for many years at the back of the second siding at Seaforth Sands, being retained for very occasional use as a snow clearance vehicle. During 1918-19 open balcony type top covers were fitted to nine of the open top cars. Nos 1, 3, 5, 7, & 8 were also fitted with canopied ends and with 180° staircases, making them more or less identical with Nos 11, 14, 15, & 16 which were similarly covered. Five of these covers came from Preston, and it is presumed that the remaining four were made by the Company. The new work on the car bodies increased the unladen weight to 10ton 1cwt.

On one or two occasions covers were changed over from one car to another; in 1923-4 for example, No. 7 was open topped and No. 6 covered, but in 1925 this situation was reversed. The fleet at closure consisted of two un-canopied open top cars, Nos 2 and 4; three canopied open top cars, Nos 6, 12, & 13 and the aforementioned more or less standardised, nine cars with both covers and canopies – Nos 1, 3, 5, 7, 8, 11, 14, 15 & 16.

The normal service operated on a six-minute frequency for the 16min journey, which required seven cars to operate, though two extra cars were put on at rush hours, each running close behind one of the scheduled cars. It appears that nine was the largest number ever in use at one time, apart from occasional peaks on Bank Holidays. The Sunday morning service was worked at half frequency, requiring four cars.

The 1911 timetable shows the service from Great Crosby starting at 5.20am running at 10min frequency until 7.50am. One car then ran at 7.45am after which the 6min service began, continuing until 5.30pm, when a 5min service operated in lieu of duplicate trams until 6.30pm, when the 6min interval resumed until 10.25pm. The service then reduced to 10min (the 11.05pm connecting with the last train to Dingle) until close down at 11.45pm. The Sunday service did not start until 10.04am. The weekday trams at 8.12am, 8.42am and 9.12am were special 'smoking cars' which connected with fast trains leaving Seaforth at 8.30am, 9.0am and 9.30am. Running in the outward direction the service was, naturally, similar, with starting times of 5.0am (weekdays) and 9.45am (Sundays). South Road the major stop for Waterloo, was exactly halfway in terms of running time. All cars worked through from one end to the other, though one instance is recorded of a car seen bearing a board on its dash announcing that it ran to South Road only.

Operating procedure was straightforward: a car arriving at the Seaforth Sands terminus would find one siding empty and a car in the other, and shortly after its arrival the other car would leave, passing other cars at the loops at Church Road, Cambridge Road, South Road, Marldon Avenue and Endbutt Lane. The other loops were needed only in case of some irregularity having occurred, which was infrequent, though cars did often have to wait a little at the loops, especially that at Marldon Avenue.

The through fare was originally 2d with one penny stages from Seaforth Sands to South Road, South Road to Great Crosby and Cambridge Road to Myers Road West. At the end of 1920 fares were raised to 3d through and 1½d per stage, the tickets remaining as before, white for a stage and crimson for a through, and always bearing the names of the stages. A through cheap return from Great Crosby or Waterloo to Liverpool by tram and Overhead Railway was also offered. The fares for this were: Great Crosby to James Street, 1st class 9d, 3rd class 7d. Waterloo to James Street, 1st class 7d and 3rd class 5d. Later a weekly return was also offered, which cost 3s 0d 1st class and 2s 0d for 3rd class from Great Crosby or 2s 8d for 1st class and 1s 8d for 3rd class and which was available for all the intermediate stations.

There was an additional concession in that the Waterloo tickets were also available to and from St. John's Road instead of South Road. Through returns were card tickets, and return halves were surrendered on the tram, the ordinary tram ticket given in exchange being punched in a special section bearing the words "St. John's Road, Railway Returns".

As early as 1904 complaints had arisen in both Waterloo and Crosby about noisy running of the cars, a defect which was attributed by Mr. Cottrell (General Manager and Engineer) to the state of the track. It appears that the local authorities were not very helpful when the Company sought any co-operation in repairs to the track or roadway, indeed only one significant improvement to the track is recorded. At College Road and at Five Lamps the road was laid with wood blocks instead of stone setts, a frequent device employed where noise from vehicle wheels was a problem. In 1921 these were relaid in stone, which gave the opportunity to renew the track at those points. By this time the Company had already requested, and been refused, a 14 years' extension of its lease, which was to expire in 1925. This seems to have engendered some quite understandable pique, as the Company had been spending quite serious money on the improvements to its cars; with the exception mentioned above, no more was spent on the track.

Right:
Car No 6 with its optional upper deck cover passing the War Memorial and Five Lamps at Waterloo c1924.

Early in 1925, when the lease was almost up, the track was mostly in poor condition, and the running of the cars was very noisy. Passenger figures and receipts were still reasonably healthy, as the following figures show.

Year	*Passengers*	*Receipts in £'s*
1919	4,578,618	
1920	4,408,793	Not
1921	3,522,092	Available
1922	3,400,207	25,860
1923	3,484,078	25,971
1924	3,593,574	26,683
1925	3,522,406	26,031

In view of the capital expenditure needed, the future was scarcely bright, and anticipating the inevitable end, the two local councils opened negotiations with Liverpool, to have the tramway linked to the City's system and the track doubled for most of the way. City trams would have had to pass under the railway bridge at Seaforth Sands, which meant that either the tramway had to be lowered, the railway bridge raised or special cars built. The Corporation Tramways solution, at least as a temporary expedient, was to use open top cars for the service, and they actually converted six old cars to clear the bridge. Presumably their intention was to acquire some or all of the LOR cars and convert these also. The plans proceeded with the installation of a Corporation traction standard and feeder box at South Road in early December 1925, but at the last moment the whole arrangement foundered on a failure to agree fares. Liverpool offered a 2d through fare from Seaforth Sands to Crosby, and 4d through from Crosby to the City. These were favourable rates, but the sticking point came, for the local councils, on the intermediate stages; intermediate stages within the City were 1d, but the Corporation would not reduce the old rate of

Above:
Exterior of the old Seaforth Sands station showing the tramway terminal on the right.

1½d. Presumably Liverpool thought that a through fares reduction of one third was quite enough to offer to the limited bargaining power of the local councils. In a sense they were wrong, for on 23 December the councils approached Waterloo and Crosby Motor Services Ltd, a firm which had been the pioneer of bus operations in the area a couple of years previous, with a route from Litherland to Crosby. With the enterprise often displayed by such firms, the bus operator had, within a week now generally spent in Yuletide revelry, obtained a small fleet of ancient buses on hire. The last tram ran on New Year's Eve, and the following day pre-war B type buses from the London General Omnibus Company began to run. By April the first of the new buses for the service had arrived, and the tramway had gone forever.

The tramcars remained in the depot for a considerable time, but were finally broken up for scrap.

8. More, Faster and Safer

The maintenance of the opening service required, at its busiest time the use of 12 trains, which left only three in reserve. In the event of any serious failure, which in view of the novel nature of the undertaking had to be regarded as a distinct possibility, the maintenance of the service could well become problematical, and while there were enterprising horse bus operators around, reliability was absolutely essential. The initial success of the services, and this realisation that the reserve capacity was of doubtful adequacy coupled with the implementation of the decision to build the Northern Extension sufficed to cause the Board to order additional stock, which they did late in 1893, again patronising the Electric Construction Corporation and Brown, Marshall & Co.

The new stock was in many respects similar to the first batch, with the electrical and mechanical parts identical, but the bodywork, although resembling the first batch in style showed a number of differences, of which the most obvious was that they were only 40ft long over the body, 42ft 6in over the buffers. Those who looked closely would also observe that the buffers were substantially larger, and of a squarer shape than those of the first batch, which had given some trouble through locking on the sharper curves of the line. The new pattern completely solved the problem, and continued to be used until the closure of the line. The overall shortening of the vehicle led to a shortening of the separation of the bogie centres by the same amount, 5ft, and made the complete motor coach some 30cwt lighter than its predecessors, at 18½tons.

The driver was released from the claustrophobic cupboard he had inhabited, and allowed to promenade across the train in a full-width cab, which must not only have made his job pleasanter but also, by improving his view, safer. Although this represented a further reduction in the effective floor space of the coach, the number of seats was not reduced, provision remaining at 41 for 2nd Class and 16 for 1st class. The saving in space was effected entirely at the expense of those who had to stand when all seats were taken. Reduced length also affected the buffer locking problem, and while existing 45ft stock was not shortened, no more new 45ft stock was built.

By 1895 the railway was benefiting from greatly increased numbers of passengers (over 7½ million in that year) and had a seat occupancy overall (excluding Bank Holidays, but including normally quiet times) of 60%, which meant that at rush hours the trains were extremely full. In addition it was anticipated that the forthcoming opening of the Southern Extension would produce yet more customers. This made the ordering of new stock necessary, and also the running of larger trains to meet the peak demands. Eight new motor coaches and eight trailer coaches were ordered from the same suppliers (though the Electric Construction Corporation had by now changed its name to The Electric Construction Co. Ltd). The new motor coaches were identical to the second batch in most respects, but being designed to handle the extra weight of a trailer coach were equipped with more powerful motors, of 70hp as against 60hp. These, although of similar design to their smaller brothers, were of increased size and weight, the motor with axle, but less wheel, now weighing 3ton 17cwt, an increase of 17cwt. The new motor bogies weighed 6ton 4cwt complete, and the total weight of electrical equipment was 6ton 17cwt. The complete motor coach rose in weight to approximately 19ton.

Bodily, they were altered only in one very noticeable respect, by the absence of any 1st class accommodation, which was transferred to the trailer cars, leaving space for 57 3rd class seats. The improvements which had been embodied in the second batch of trains were, of course, retained. A curious anomaly existed in the numbering of the motor coaches of this batch, in that while Nos 41 & 42 were built in 1896, Nos 39 & 40 were not built until 1897. One possible explanation for this is that the actual interval between their deliveries was not very long, and that the new stock was left lined up on the same road until the batch was ready for service and then numbered from the front instead of from the back, thus reversing the order in which they arrived.

Above:
A standard three-car train entering Gladstone Dock station. *Real Photographs Co*

The trailer coaches, which were numbered as a separate series, were substantially shorter than the motors at 32ft overall, 34ft 6in over the buffers, which gave them a somewhat stumpy appearance. In most respects they resembled their motorised counterparts, using similar bogies, mounted at 20ft centres, but they differed in having the usual Westinghouse braking system applied to all axles instead of only three. These first trailers were fitted out for 1st class passengers only, for whom they provided 40 seats. The weight of the trailers complete was 13ton 2cwt.

The eight trailers made possible the running of eight three-car trains, leaving 15 two-car trains. Obviously this meant that four of the three-car trains would have to operate with motors of the first or second batches which had only 60hp to drive them. Further, the 70hp units were found a little short on power, with the result that over a period most of the motor coaches for three-car trains were re-equipped with two ECC motors each, mounted on the second and third axles.

In January 1901 the Company scored another first, when they brought a Reno escalator into service at Seaforth Sands Station. While there had been a number of successful installations in the United States, including one at Brooklyn Bridge in 1896 and another shortly afterwards on the Manhattan Elevated Railway, it appears that the first in England was that exhibited at Crystal Palace in 1899, which means that the one at Seaforth was the second erected, and the first for normal public use. It was also, of course, the first railway escalator. It took the form of an endless belt rising at the angle of a normal staircase, with a rubber handrail running at the same speed of 100ft per minute. Operated by an electric motor of 10hp, it had a capacity of 3,500 passengers per hour.

Although it was a highly significant innovation, it appears not to have been a great success, largely because it had a number of exposed moving parts which made a habit of damaging clothing. The Company received many claims for such damage, especially from female passengers, the majority of whom tended to wear clothing which might be charitably described as voluminous, and the result was that when the new Seaforth Sands Station was built in 1906 (see below) the opportunity was taken quietly to forget about the escalator. It was probably the last escalator built until the Earls Court Exhibition of 1911, where one was erected upon which the public might ride for a fare of ½d.

28

27

Nº
44
Nº
45

Left:
A three-car train of wide bodied stock at Seaforth and Litherland. *C. E. Box*

Below left:
A three-car train of the original stock as widened and rebuilt in 1902/3. *C. E. Box*

Bottom left:
A comparison of the widened and standard bodies on Nos 44 and 45 respectively.
C. E. Box

Shortly after that escalators began to appear on the London Underground, where they developed into the almost unavoidable feature of urban travel that they have now become.

The Company had improved the performance of its trains, and was flirting with more new ideas, but these developments were not sufficient to meet a new challenge which was emerging. At the opening of the railway Sir William Forwood and others had spoken glowingly of the future for electric traction: it now reared its head in a form rather less welcome. On 16 November 1898 the first Liverpool electric tramcar ran, and the route on which it was chosen it should do so was in immediate competition with the Overhead Railway, running from St. George's Church (now demolished: the Victoria Monument, Derby Square stands on its site) to Dingle. By the end of 1900 there were also tramcars running between Pierhead and Seaforth Sands Station. These represented competition of an altogether more formidable kind than did anything pulled by a horse, though it would be interesting to know why routes were chosen at such an early stage which were in direct competition with an existing service. The effect on the railway's passenger figures was not disastrous, indeed the slackening in the rate of increase was quite slight, but the rate of increase of the passengers using the trams was so extraordinarily high that the Company could not possibly ignore the threat posed. In 1898 the electric trams carried 785,064 passengers, in 1899 15,853,160, and in 1900 an astonishing 58,068,531. Such a rate of growth could not long be sustained, but it was for one further year, with the 100 million journeys mark passed in 1901. Perhaps the members of the Board were aware of the reasons for the decline of canals: whether they were or not they determined that they must act in a decisive manner.

In March 1901 they resolved to investigate how and to what extent they could speed up their service, rightly considering that their unimpeded track and proper railway working methods could give them a decisive speed advantage over the enemy below. Dick, Kerr & Co. Ltd, of Preston, later better known as builders of trams, guaranteed that they could so equip trains as to run the whole distance from Seaforth Sands to Dingle in 20.9min, including 16 stops of 12 seconds each. This represented an increase in the overall average speed from 12½mph to nearly 19mph, an increase whose magnitude is emphasised when it is borne in mind that the fastest elevated railway in the world at the time was the Southside Elevated Railway in Chicago, with an average speed of only 14.6mph. The effect of the new service in terms of time saved was to cut the journey time 11.1min from its original 32min.

The train chosen for the installation of the experimental equipment was 41-2-42, which had already undergone one conversion job, with the fitting of roller bearings by the Roller Bearing Company. It had been shown by the falling weight test that this train would start from rest with an 80% reduction in starting effort as compared with a train equipped with plain bearings. Much more was to come, however, when Sydney Short of English Electric, who were acting as sub-contractors for Dick, Kerr, set about the task of designing entirely new electrical equipment.

At the heart of the conversion was a completely new motor, entirely contained in a rigid fire and waterproof casting which also served as the magnetic circuit for the fields and to provide really rigid support for the armature and axle bearings. The only opening in this casting was over the commutator and brushes to which access might be needed more frequently, but even this was closed with a hinged lid with robust fastenings. More serious maintenance could be undertaken by splitting the casting around a horizontal joint face, when the upper half could be removed, leaving the lower half supported on the axles and on the nose suspension. A similar technique for rendering the field and armature accessible for inspection or repair was employed in tramcar motors, where the lower half was let down into the inspection pit, but these motors were so much larger that such an arrangement would have been impractical. Inside the casting were four laminated steel pole pieces, each with

Above:
Motor car No 39. *C. E. Box*

its own field spool. These were made of copper ribbon some 2in wide, wound with asbestos and mica strip between layers and insulated outside with mica and asbestos combination boxes held in position by means of heavy braided tape. The complete coils were treated with a waterproof insulating compound and thoroughly baked. Each coil had exactly the same number of turns of copper wound onto it and was rigidly fastened to the outer shell by means of large bolts so that the field in which the armature rotated was perfectly symmetrical.

The armature was iron clad, wound with copper bars let into deep slots. Each coil was made with only one turn, so that the only joints were those at the commutator. Insulation was by a combination of mica and asbestos, treated with a specially prepared insulating varnish, and again taped up and baked. The coils were both detachable and interchangeable, so that the replacement of a damaged one was a comparatively easy operation. High grade steel was used for the cores, which ensured low hysteresis losses, and the laminations were thoroughly insulated one from another to prevent the induction of eddy currents. Built into the armature was a carefully worked out ventilation system, which carried cooling air right to the inside of the armature core through ducts to the surface.

Commutation was perfect even at double normal load, which happy state of affairs was attributable to a very large commutator made up with numerous bars. At the top were the brushes, in two pairs. Each brush was fitted by means of a brass clamp which moved with it and a flexible braided copper ribbon connected it directly with the brush holder and with the main cables from the controller, thus avoiding the transmission of current through any sliding contact faces. Resulting from such attention to detail was a characteristic curve revealing an efficiency of well over 90%. Against the standard of a temperature rise of 70°C after one hour's running at full load, the new motor showed a rise at the commutator of 55°, at the armature of 39°, at the fields of 57° and at the bearings of only 14° at the pinion end and 9° at the commutator end.

It was not only in their electrical arrangements that the new motors varied from previous practice however, for they were no longer built direct onto the axles, but drove through gearing. Despite the results of experiments with roller bearings for axles, plain bearings were retained for the motors, provided with both oil and grease lubrication. A recycling system was provided to catch and return oil which emerged from the ends of the bearings. The pinion was of hammered machine steel, and the gears were machined from a cast blank: both were enclosed by an oil-tight malleable iron casing. The motor weighed 3,945lb, and the complete assembly including gears, housing etc. totalled 4,387lb, which was a mere 43.8lb per horsepower. The method of motor mounting was also new, to diminish shock transmission to the permanent way, and consisted of a journal mount at one end of the driving axle,

with a spring mount to the bogie frame on the other side.

With the new motors came a new control system, known as Type Q4, form D, capable of carrying up to 800A, which remained in use right through to the closure of the line. The circuits they controlled involved fairly regular making and breaking at a current of 700A, for four of the new 100hp motors, and to prevent excessive arcing at the contacts magnetic blow-out coils were fitted. These devices had been patented by Thorsten Von Zweigbergk, of Cleveland, Ohio (US Patent 22,250, 28 September 1897) and consisted of a long coil of copper tape wound on a straight iron core which extended from top to bottom of the controller. Enclosing it was an outer tube of copper on which were mounted the contact pieces and also projecting discs of insulating material, which divided the whole assembly into a series of little compartments within each of which the make and break was effected. The whole assembly was mounted on pivots, so that it could be swung out for inspection or cleaning: it was in some respects the most important part of the controller, for on its efficient working depended the survival of the contacts.

The controller had two handles on it. The smaller was the master switch, which had seven positions: a central "off" position and the following alternatives; all motors ahead; all motors reverse; motors 1 & 2 ahead; 1 & 2 reverse; 3 & 4 ahead; 3 & 4 reverse. The larger lever was known as the power handle, and was equipped with a locking plunger to ensure that it located positively in each notch. It was also interlocked with the master switch, so that it could only be moved when the latter was in one of the running positions, which was to protect the master switch from being used to make or break heavy currents. The positions of the power handle began with motors 1 & 3 and 2 & 4 in parallel pairs, the two pairs wired in series, with the magnetic blow out and 6 resistances in circuit. The next three notches left the motors unaltered, but progressively reduced the resistance to zero and cut out the magnetic blow out. There followed three transitional notches, which had to be passed through quickly, of which the first reconnected the blow out and half the resistance, the second took out one set of motors and the third disconnected one set of motors and half the resistance ready for reconnection in the parallel notches which followed. These were again three in number, connecting all motors in parallel and respectively all resistances, half the resistances, and finally the full speed notch, with no resistances and no blow out.

Apart from the robust nature of the motor casing, a number of other measures were incorporated to minimise the risk of fire, including the lining of the driver's compartment and all woodwork in the vicinity of electrical components with "Uralite" and encasing all cables in iron troughs. Such precautions would, of course, have prevented the disastrous Dingle fire described in Chapter 9.

Above:
Motor car No 40. *C. E. Box*

The trials of the experimental train were highly successful, and seemed amply to justify the expense of their greater power consumption. In series without resistances a peak current of 600A was drawn, while in full parallel the current was 700A. This produced, however, not only a top speed of 32mph, but also an impressive time for acceleration from 0-30mph of 40 seconds. Lengthy tests were conducted by Mr Cottrell, the General Manager and Chief Engineer in conjunction with Mr Mallock of Dick, Kerr, and it was clearly established that the train could make the journey easily in under 20½minutes. The actual rate of acceleration achieved was 4.2ft/second^2, nearly 3mph per second and braking proved equally effective at a deceleration of 4.75ft/second^2. On the basis of this undoubtedly tram-beating performance, Dick, Kerr were given the contract to re-equip the whole of the rolling stock after the manner of the experimental train with only a few minor alterations.

Right:
Car No 39 in the new carriage sheds.
C. E. Box

Below right:
First class trailer coach No 3. *C. E. Box*

The high performance of the experimental train is perhaps more easily appreciated when it is compared with the service speeds of some other urban railways. In each case the speed quoted is in miles per hour average over the journey, including stops.

Liverpool Overhead	19
South Side Elevated (Chicago)	14.6
Metropolitan Elevated	14.5
Central London	14.0
Manhattan Elevated	13.5
Lake Street Elevated (Chicago)	12.5
City and South London	12.5

The running times were as follows:

'Up Trains'

Seaforth Sands
Alexandra, 2 minutes
Langton, 3 minutes
Brocklebank, 3½ minutes
Canada, 5 minutes
Huskisson, 6 minutes
Nelson, 7½ minutes
Clarence, 8½ minutes
Princes, 10 minutes
Pier Head, 11½ minutes
James Street, 12½ minutes
Custom House, 13½ minutes
Wapping, 14½ minutes
Brunswick, 16 minutes
Toxteth, 17¼ minutes
Herculaneum, 18¼ minutes
Dingle, 20 minutes

'Down Trains'

Dingle
Herculaneum, 1½ minutes
Toxteth, 3 minutes
Brunswick, 4 minutes
Wapping, 5 minutes
Custom House, 6 minutes
James Street, 7 minutes
Pier Head, 8 minutes
Princes, 9½ minutes
Clarence, 11 minutes
Nelson, 12 minutes
Huskisson, 13½ minutes
Canada, 14½ minutes
Brocklebank, 16 minutes
Langton, 17 minutes
Alexandra, 18 minutes
Seaforth Sands, 20 minutes

The first 'up' train on weekdays departed Seaforth Sands at 4.45am
The last 'up' train on weekdays departed Seaforth Sands, at 11.30pm
The first 'down' train on weekdays departed Dingle 5.0am
The last 'down' train on weekdays departed Dingle 11.25pm
The first 'up' train on Sundays departed Seaforth Sands 9.5am
The last 'up' train on Sundays departed Seaforth Sands 11.50pm
The first 'down' train on Sundays departed Dingle 9.15am
The last 'down' train on Sundays departed Dingle 11.25pm

In the contract for the re-equipment the use of roller bearings was again eschewed, despite the successful trials, and one or two changes were made which had not appeared on the prototype, of which perhaps the most significant was the use of larger wheels, at 3ft in place of 2ft 9in, although the gearing remained the same. The gears were of 48 teeth and the pinions of 17, giving a ratio of 2.82:1. The new driver's compartment was, like that in the second batch of stock, full width, and the frontal appearance was very noticeably altered by the substitution of a solid panel for the middle front window. This had the circuit breaker mounted on the inside and the car number painted in large white letters on a red ground on the outside. In the next panel was mounted an electric lamp which served for head or rear by the insertion or removal of a red glass slide: these remained a distinctive feature until the introduction of the final generation of modernised stock.

The extra power of the new motors encouraged the Company to have ten of the original 45ft motor coaches rebuilt by Brown Marshall & Co with a widened body. The increase seemed slight enough, a mere 10in from 8ft 6in to 9ft 4in, but it was sufficient to allow five passengers instead of four to sit crosswise whilst still leaving a full length gangway. The driver retained an even wider full width compartment, and the seating capacity which resulted was 60 second class and 19 first class. The ten coaches chosen for the treatment were 6, 7, 17, 19, 20, 25 and 27 converted in 1902, and 4, 21 and 23 the following year. In the interests of aesthetics these were run as two-car trains only until the building

L.O.R

Left:
Interior of Seaforth Works showing access to the workshops below. *C. E. Box*

Below left:
Bogie showing the mounting of a 75hp motor. *C. E. Box*

Bottom left:
The interior of third class carriage in 1935. *C. E. Box*

Below:
The interior of a first class carriage in 1935. *C. E. Box*

of wide trailers 10, 11, 47 and 48 in 1917 and 1918.

It will be recalled that the enlargement of capacity in the generating station in 1900 was partly aimed at providing extra power for the Accelerated Train Service, but when the service began in September 1902 it soon manifested other troubles than a heavy electricity consumption. The power of the new motors was a little much for the transmission gearing, which stripped in a number of cases, hot bearings were a frequent problem and the higher speeds run over rails which were somewhat past the first flush of youth led to corrugation and axle failures. By 1908 it was clear that the new units were simply too powerful for their own good, and the somewhat basic step was taken of affixing a seal which prevented the power handle being moved into the parallel notches. This, of course, reduced the speed considerably, but did not make savings in current nearly commensurate with that reduction. The Company was thus left with something of a white elephant until 1919, when the decision was taken to re-motor once again.

It is, of course, possible that the decision to reduce the performance may have been connected with personal bêtes noires, for it was in that year the Mr Cottrell left the Company, and was replaced by his Chief Assistant Edward Neachell. Electrical engineering was still a small world then, and Mr Neachell had served his apprenticeship with ECC of Wolverhampton, contractor to the LOR. Later he had entered the firm's laboratory, being responsible for testing of a variety of equipment for railways, tramways and lighting plant, including the new generating station for the City and South London Railway, opened in 1900. In 1901 he went to work for the English Electric Manufacturing Company as Electrical and Mechanical Engineer, where he was responsible for the equipment of a number of tramways, including those of Grimsby, Cleethorpes and Portsmouth. In 1903, the same year that EEM was taken over by Dick, Kerr, he left them to join the Overhead. He was an active 'Institute' man, being elected an associate of the Institute of Mechanical Engineers in 1903 (member in 1908) and also a member of the Institution of Electrical Engineers and of the Liverpool Engineering Society.

In 1905 some new stock had appeared on the Overhead which was not of their own design, or indeed ownership, for it was built by the Lancashire and Yorkshire Railway in order that they could run through services from Southport to Dingle and from Aintree to Dingle. These

trains were special lightweight multiple units, made up of twelve cars whose bodies were built at Newton Heath Carriage Works, incorporating electrical components by Dick, Kerr. The bodies were 45ft long and 9ft 6in wide with aluminium exterior panelling and fittings and inset doors (though they were later built with flush doors). The bogies mounted one 125hp geared motor each, driving 3ft 6in wheels on a wheelbase of 7ft, their own mounting centres being separated by 32ft. At 12ft 3⅞in from rail to the top of the roof they were markedly tall by LOR standards, and at 22ton a little heavy, and they must have been comparatively spacious, for they carried almost as many seated passengers (20 for first and 50 for third class) per car as the LOR wide-bodied stock. Clearly there was not sufficient demand all year round for through working to justify six trains, and for many years they were also used to maintain a regular service between Southport and Crossens. Their L&YR numbers had been 1000 to 1011, changing at the grouping to LMSR 11700 to 11711. They were eventually broken up in 1940 at the LMSR electric car works, Meols Cop.

The availability of more powerful motors together with the very heavy use of trains at rush hours, a gently rising number of passengers overall and the difficulty of diminishing the headway led to a decision to convert gradually to operation based entirely on three car trains. The first step in implementing this policy was the building, in 1914 of a new standard 1st class trailer to replace No. 5, the car destroyed in the Dingle fire, and this was followed in 1916 by No. 9 built by Metropolitan-Cammel Carriage and Wagon Co. In 1917 two wide trailers were built for the first class, again by Metropolitan-Cammel, numbered 10 & 11, while the same builder produced, in the following year, two third class trailers which rode on 3ft wheels and were of the same length (45ft) as the motor coaches, these being Nos 47 & 48. Curiously, a fifth wide trailer was never built, so that one train, 7-16-9, went through life looking rather odd with wide motors and a standard trailer.

Conversion to all-three-car working now suffered something of an hiatus, for no further trailers were built, and when extra trailers were required, as in 1926 for the new workman's trains, motor coaches were pressed into service. These trains had a total unladen weight of 55

Above:
The interior of the modernised third class carriage. *C. E. Box*

Above right:
The interior of the modernised first class carriage. *C. E. Box*

Centre right:
The second train of the modernised stock, No 16, which was completed in 1947, at Seaforth and Litherland station. *C. E. Box*

Below right:
The LOR machine shop and smithy at Seaforth in 1924. The old tram shed can be seen through the end doors against which is a portable track welder.

For all ADVERTISING
ON THE
OVERHEAD

CIRCLE
16

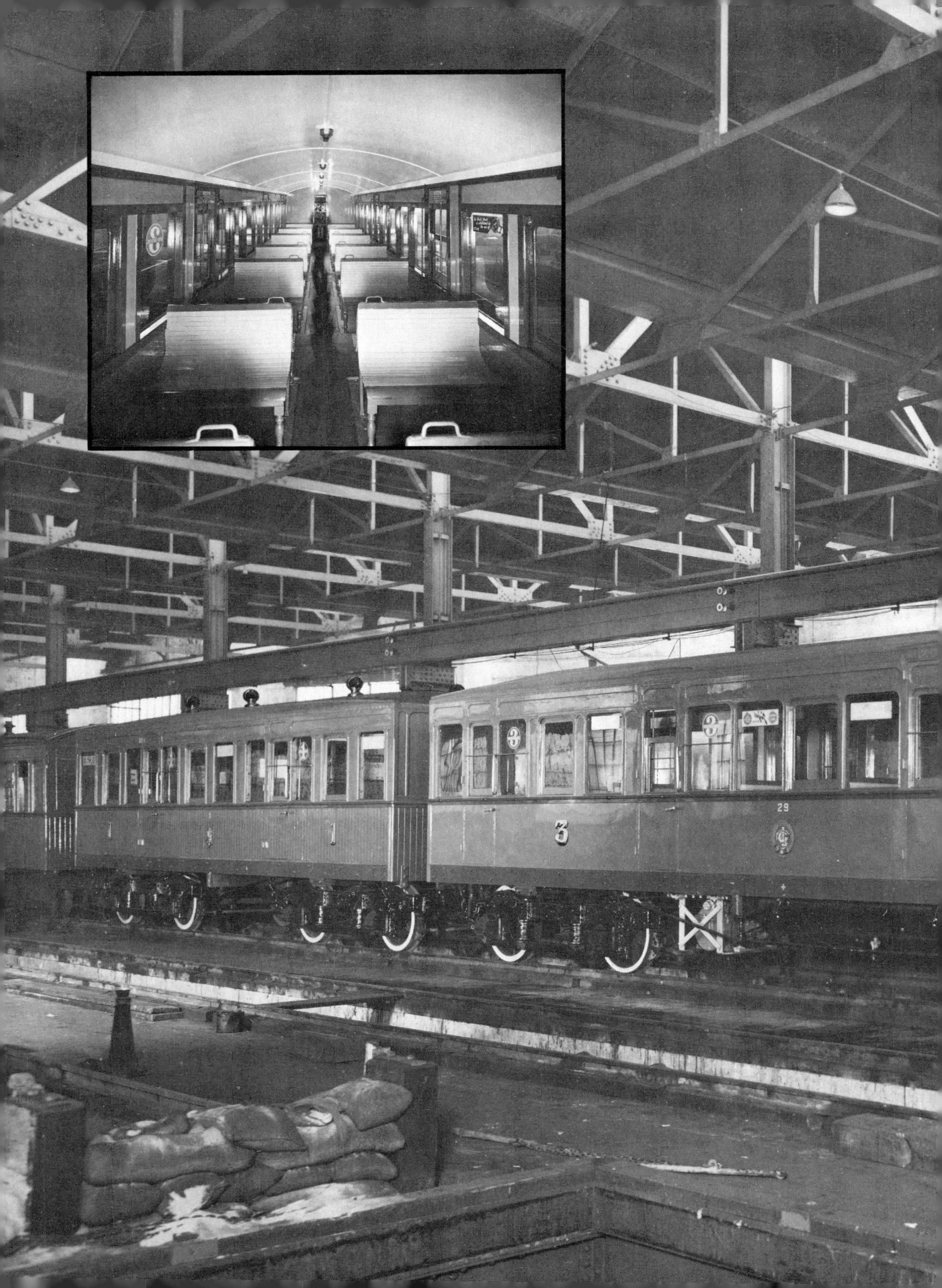
3
29

Below:
Rebuilt motor-coach No 29 in the carriage works in January 1945.

Left:
An interior view of the rebuilt motor-coach No 29.

tons, and seated 56 in each motor and 64 in a trailer. A total of 176 per train, plus of course as many as could get in to stand. The coaches making up the trains were 1-22-9 and 11-14-16, but during 1931-2 they were reconstructed as standard stock. 1932 also saw the beginning of the final stage of conversion to all-three-car-working, with the conversion of motor No. 38 to a standard trailer, renumbered 12. Nos 13-17 followed, being similar conversions from, respectively, motors 31, 33, 37, 34, and 36. 13 and 14 emerged in their new state in 1933 and the remaining three in the three following years. All the conversion work was done in the Seaforth Carriage Shed, by the Company's own staff.

Meanwhile, in 1926, Mr Neachell had retired from his post of General Manager and Engineer. Senior positions in the LOR do not seem to have improved life expectancy, for he died in 1934 at the early age of 61. His post was divided, William Grundy being appointed General Manager the same year. He came of an old railway family, and had begun his career in the Bingley Goods Depot of the Midland Railway in 1891, where his father was the stationmaster. He

Above:
Seaforth new works under construction and also showing the old station being demolished and the new one on the right. *F. Wood & Co*

Above right:
View of the new works as completed.
D. Fox & Partners

worked in both the Goods and Passenger departments there, and then joined the District Goods Manager's Department at Leeds, serving for some years as a relief clerk.

He was largely responsible for the construction of the Sand Hutton Light Railway, of which he was a Director. (Situated about eight miles north east of York this was a 15in gauge line, later enlarged to 18in, which opened in 1910). In 1911 he was appointed Chief Clerk at the London North Western/Midland joint station at Morecambe, but remained only three years before taking up the post of General Manager and Accountant of the Derwent Valley Light Railway, where he remained until his

appointment to the LOR. In 1920 he had been nominated by the Minister of Transport, Sir Eric Geddes, to serve on a committee to examine and report on the future policies possible towards light railways with reference both to operation and construction, and in 1925 he was elected a member of the Institute of Transport. 1926 saw his appointment as a member of the Light Railway Advisory Committee.

It is evident that despite his very wide and varied experience, Mr Grundy was no engineer, and the position of Chief Engineer was filled by the promotion of the former assistant engineer, Wilfred Box.

Long before the conversion to three-car operation was complete it had become necessary to begin a similar rolling programme to replace motors, for the 100hp motors were nearing the end of their useful life, and in any case the limitation to series-only running which had been placed on them rendered them highly inefficient. In 1920 therefore, the decision was taken to replace them with 75hp motors, capable of running in full parallel, which would not only reduce current consumption, but also give a faster service. The new motors also gave a considerable saving in weight, weighing only 1 ton (2,240lb), compared with the 3,945lb of the old units. The gear ratio was considerably reduced which was a great advantage in saving strain on the structure, particularly where elderly and hammered rail joints were involved and on the curves (which accounted for 1/16 of the whole length of the line) where the centrifugal strains were reduced. The gear ratios were reduced, from 2.82:1 to 4.2:1 by the use of new gears of 70 teeth meshing with pinions of 17. During the successful trials of the new motors, one piece of slightly peripheral information on lubrication costs was gathered, which established that one train had its axle boxes (24 bearings) lubricated with 17 pints of oil and on another occasion with only 16½. The price of oil then being 2 shillings per gallon, this gave a lubrication cost of rather less than ½d per 1,000 miles, which must have been equalled by few railways.

In 1920 trains were classified in three types. The remaining two-car trains were made up from stock which still had the old 100hp motors, which gave (from two motors) a tractive effort of

6,000lb on starting, 7,600lb at one-hour rating. The maximum starting current was 250A, and maximum speed on the level was 30mph, with 20.5mph at one-hour rating. These were known as Class A; Class B being the remaining three-car trains driven by four of the old motors, for which the corresponding figures were: tractive effort starting, 12,000lb, 7,600 at one-hour rating; maximum current at starting 500A; maximum speed 32mph, with 20.5 at one-hour rating. The new 75hp motors were used only in three-car trains, known as Class C, which, owing to their lower gearing, had quite different characteristics, with a tractive effort of 13,000lb at starting and 8,000lb at one-hour rating. The starting current ceiling was 400A, and the maximum train speed 20mph, with 14.5mph at one-hour rating. In practice the average running current of a train worked out at about 120A, irrespective of its class, with the starting current usually between 300A and 500A. The load in first parallel notch was often about the same as the starting current. Drivers were equipped with an ammeter, which read 0-1000A in most of the trains, though some read 0-800A.

The average train speeds on the level, including stops, were 14mph for two-car trains and 13mph for three cars, but it is worth recording an occasion one Sunday morning in July 1934 when my father and I accompanied a

Above left:
Exterior view of Seaforth Sands works, the signal box and the station. *C. E. Box*

Left:
One of the LMSR 'Dingle' trains at Pier Head station. *J. B. Horne*

Above:
Another view of an LMSR Dingle' train on the LOR. *C. E. Box*

driver in his cab between Seaforth Sands and Pier Head, a trip which was normally booked to be covered in ten minutes for a non-stop run over the 3 miles 1578 yds. On this particular occasion the distance was covered in almost exactly eight minutes, a start-to-stop average of 29.22mph, which was achieved by the driver remaining in full parallel for virtually the entire trip. The centrifugal strain on the structure through the curves at Alexandra must have been immense: a consideration which led to the driver being carpeted next day for excessive speed.

No distinction was made in the classification between wide and normal stock, so that weights cannot be quoted by class. Two-car trains of standard stock weighed 40ton unladen, 47ton 2½cwt with all seats occupied, and 51ton 5cwt fully loaded (allowing for 66 standing passengers). The wide two-car trains were 42ton unladen, 62ton 14cwt with their 160 seats occupied, and 67ton 14½cwt fully laden, allowing 66 passengers standing. Three-car standard trains weighed 53ton 12cwt unladen, 62ton 14½cwt with 154 seated passengers and 67ton 14¼cwt with a further 81 passengers standing. The juggernaut of the line was the three-car wide train, which weighed 57ton unladen, rising to 70ton 2½cwt with its 210 seated passengers, and to 75ton 3¾cwt with an additional 81 passengers standing.

While these alterations in stock had been proceeding, other aspects of the company's operations had also required modification as the years went by, not least among which was the signalling system. Although the original automatic signalling systems had worked satisfactorily, it was felt desirable to introduce further safeguards, and in 1897 the signalling of trains from one intermediate station to the next by means of the W.R. Sykes semaphore-bell block instrument was introduced, in conjunction with lock and block instruments at the termini. Although the installation was made at the suggestion of the Board of Trade, the suggestion was not based on any accidents which had occurred, but merely on a desire to keep the signalling up to date. The instruments employed were a modification of the old Sykes double arm block instrument as originally employed on the London Chatham and Dover Railway. The arms of the instrument were normally down, and came up when a train was on the section: adjoining the arms was a small frame which housed a plate bearing station names. Each station now kept a train book in which was entered the time at which the signals were received for "Be ready", "train on line", and "line clear" so that any error would be readily traceable. A final precaution lay in the fact that every station had a telephone, and the General Manager's Office could thus communicate with any of them.

The original signal system proved to have one significant disadvantage, which was the cost of maintaining the 50V batteries, and as a consequence maintenance was not always perfect: this in turn led to signal failures brought about by voltage drop. In 1902, Mr Cottrell began a series of experiments aimed at operating the signals from the traction supply. His prototype signal replaced the old contact box with a bar placed in the four foot. The equivalent of the old break contact, which set the signal to danger was a bar which was so placed as to be depressed by the passing train, while the new "make" contact was a bar placed such that it was energised by the twin collector shoe of the passing train with current from the conductor rail. The operation of the signals was otherwise exactly as in the original installation, and the only other modifications made, the replacement of the mercury arm contacts with mechanical arm contacts and the use of the running rail in place of the common return wire likewise had no effect on the actual principles employed. The experimental set-up was entirely successful, with such beneficial effect that within a year all signals had been converted to the new arrangement. Not only did this reduce the running costs in obvious respects by abolishing the batteries, but it also simplified the wiring and switchgear considerably, with the result that other faults became less likely and also easier to diagnose and rectify if they should occur.

From a low point in 1909, the volume of passengers had been steadily increasing, breaking the ten million mark in 1913 for the first time in 13 years. The following year, in order to increase the capacity of the line by allowing for closer headway, the longer sections between stations (those between Brocklebank and Canada, Clarence and Princes, Custom House and Wapping and Wapping and Brunswick) were each equipped with outer home signals, situated 200 yds in rear of the inner home signals. This alteration was no doubt prophetic of the baleful increase in traffic brought about by the Great War. How many men took their last journey on an English railway 16ft above the Dock Road before embarking on a one-way trip to the Western Front?

In 1917 a further safety precaution was added in the shape of the electric train stop, which was fitted to all the automatic starting and outer home signals. An earthing bar, insulated from the main structure, was mounted in the four foot just in advance of the signal. If the driver attempted to pass with the signal at danger a wire brush, connected to the controller side of the main switch contacted the bar. This made the circuit which energised a solenoid, the armature of which tripped the automatic main switch and also opened the emergency cock on the air brake system, bringing the train to a halt. When the signal was set clear the contacts on the signal arm opened the circuit through the bar to earth, allowing the train to pass unmolested.

Unfortunately these additional precautions did not suffice to prevent two fairly minor accidents within weeks of each other in 1919, on 13 January and 12 February, and the report of Colonel Pringle, of the Board of Trade on the accidents attributed them largely to the inadequacy of the signalling system for the handling of trains on a 2½ minute service. He recommended that the original system be scrapped, and replaced with an entirely new and up-to-date installation embodying track circuiting. This system had been invented by an American, William Robinson, in 1872, and its use had spread rapidly on American railways during the 1880s. The first use of track circuits in England was an experimental system installed by W. R. Sykes at Crystal Palace Station in 1876, but this was not successful, and it was not until 1886 that the first permanent installation was made at St. Paul's (Blackfriars).

The first practical, rather than experimental, use of track circuiting in this country was on the London & South Western Railway, between Grateley and Andover, in 1901, and by 1910 the system was sufficiently established to feature as a recommendation in Colonel Pringle's report on the Hawes Junction accident. Thus by 1919 sufficient experience had been gained for the Company to make enquiries of three different firms, who were each allocated a trial section of the line on which to set up the system they proposed, and these were inspected by Major Hall on 27 January 1920. He made his

Above right:
Breaking up a Dingle coach at Meols Cop, Electric Car Works. Southport in 1940.

Right:
The semaphore signals at Seaforth, shown here in a 1920s view, remained until the closure of the line.
C. E. Box

recommendations to the Ministry of Transport (which had, as of 15 August 1919, taken over responsibility for railway safety from the Board of Trade) and after approval had been given the Company accepted the tender of McKenzie Holland and Westinghouse Power Signal Co. Ltd, (now the Westinghouse Brake and Signal Co. Ltd of Chippenham). This tender, which was dated 12 March 1920, was for the supply and installation of automatic and semi-automatic signalling on the ordinary overlap system between Alexandra and Herculaneum at a cost of £19,710. The signal boxes and mechanical signalling had been allowed to remain at the ends of the line, hence the exclusion of Dingle and Seaforth Sands from the tender.

The principle employed was that when a train passed a signal it set it to danger, and the signal remained so set until the whole length of the train was clear of the section. At one stage it was considered necessary to ensure that two consecutive sections were unoccupied before a signal would clear, but this was found to be a greater margin than was really needed. It was deemed sufficient to allow a signal to clear when a train had passed into the next section by a distance sufficient for a following train to come to rest should it pass a signal at danger, under the action of the automatic train stop. This distance, known as the overlap, was determined by practical experiment and found to be 300ft. In one or two instances it was necessary to increase this figure owing to a signal being sited on a falling gradient.

Below:
The exterior of the signal box at Seaforth. *C. E. Box*

Right:
A typical single lever. *C. E. Box*

Above:
The interior of the signal box at Seaforth.
C. E. Box

Each station was protected by a home signal a little more than one overlap's length in the rear and a starter immediately in advance. In general these allowed a train to enter a station as soon as the previous train had entered the next station; the latter being protected by the signal in the rear of the station and its overlap. It was also permissible for the following train to leave its station, passing the starter at clear. Further, it could proceed to the next station while the previous train was still in the following section as that was by then under the protection of the next starter and its overlap. This allowed very close headways, the system being intended for a two-minute service, although the calculations of the signal positions provided an extra margin of safety by being based on a 100 second service. The manner in which these positions were determined was based on a scale plan of the line. By experiment, the typical duration of station stops was obtained, and found to be as follows: Alexandra 25 seconds; Brocklebank 25; Canada 28; Huskisson 25; Nelson 20; Clarence 20; Princes 20; Pier Head 30; James Street 25; Custom House 20; Wapping 20; Brunswick 20; Toxteth 20 and Herculaneum 25 seconds. When to these figures were added an average speed of 20mph, an acceleration on leaving stations of 1.1 ft/sec^2 and a deceleration on approaching stations of 2ft/sec^2 it became possible to plot on the plan the position of a train at any stage in its journey. Given that each station required a home signal to protect a train standing in it and a starter signal to protect the previous train when a train was leaving it, it was possible to draw vertical ordinates on the plan which revealed whether, when a train was approaching any signal, there was no other train in the section which that signal controlled. Thus any proposed siting of a signal could be proved right or wrong immediately.

Running trains so close together required a thoroughly efficient train stop, as this might well be the only safeguard remaining after a driver error. The normal type, as used on the London electric railways was not applicable owing to the longitudinal sleepers on the LOR, and a special type attached to the rails was therefore provided, similar in construction to the type used with an electrically operated semaphore signal. The stop turned towards the rails when the signal controlling it was at danger, in which position the trip valve lever of the train would strike it. When this occurred the brakes were applied and also, as in the previous design, the main circuit breaker was opened, cutting off the supply to the motors. When the signal was set to clear a standard Westinghouse type G signal machine (telemotor) turned the stop clear of the path of the trip.

The signals represented yet another first for the LOR, the new two aspect colour light signals being the first long range daylight signal system employed in this country. Each signal had three compartments, the upper containing the equipment for the danger indication, the middle that for clear and the bottom the transformers and terminal boards. Each signal lamp had two bulbs, one requiring 12V (actually under-run at 11V), the other 110V. The inner lens of each lamp, whether red or green was made to a close specification to ensure a true and durable colour. The smaller (12V) bulb was placed at the focal point of the lens, so that the light emerged almost as a parallel beam, and each signal was carefully tested for focus in the shops and when satisfactory was sealed before despatch. Behind the 12V bulb was the 110V bulb which formed a standby in the event of the focal lamp failing. A deflecting prismatic lens could be added to deflect the beam where a signal had to be placed at a sharp curve. Outside of the coloured lens was mounted an outer lens of clear glass.

The power supply originated in the Company's power station, whence it was distributed to the stations along the line at a pressure of 600V, ac at 50 cycles. At each station transformers reduced the voltage to 100V supply to the signals and train stops. A second transformer fed its output at 6V through special regulating resistances mounted in front of the transformers to the track circuits. To the right of this assembly, on certain stations there stood a booster transformer which compensated for voltage drop in the main supply cable. Each signal was equipped with a two element vane relay on a spring mounting and enclosed within a weatherproof cast-iron box: this type of relay was chosen for its immunity from interference by the DC traction current.

Installed by Westinghouse, the new equipment in the power station consisted of two separate sets of motor alternators built by the Lancashire Dynamo & Motor Co. Ltd, who also made the associated boards and switchgear. Each machine had a dc motor driven from the normal 500V output of the main generators and was controlled by its own separate panel on the board. It drove an alternator of the rotating armature type through a direct coupling, with an output of 25kVA at 600V. One set was normally sufficient to meet all the demands of the signalling system, the second set being on standby. Particular care had been given to the design of the alternators to achieve the minimum possible variation both in voltage and in frequency, as both were fairly critical to the proper functioning of the system, and considerable success was achieved in this, despite the fact that the alternators were excited from the normal DC busbars in the power station where the acceptable variation in voltage was much higher. From the power station, the main feeder divided north and south, the cables being continuous through the whole of the automatically signalled portion of the track. At each station they were run into the tranformer casings and then out again, this enabling a physical junction to be made which in turn made it possible to test any length of cable between transformers, the latter being isolated from the mains by the 600V fuses.

There were crossover roads at Alexandra and Herculaneum and emergency crossovers at Canada, Clarence, Pier Head and Brunswick, which were not protected in the same way as the stations, but by a semi-automatic system. On the station platform was a lever which operated the crossover, and this, by means of electrical contacts attached to it, set the appropriate signals to danger, an electrical indicator on the lever confirming that the signals had responded. The signals remained at danger until the lever was returned to its normal position.

Each of the signal boxes was equipped with an illuminated diagram, with indicator lights. At Seaforth these were lit when a section was unoccupied by a train, but went out when a train entered the section, while at Dingle the lights were out when the section was clear and on when it was occupied. The retention of the mechanical signalling, which made the problems of controlling access to Seaforth and Herculaneum Carriage sheds much simpler, made for a busy life for the signalman, the following table indicating the number of lever movements to be made during a normal 16 hour weekday, worked by two 8 hour shifts.

Seaforth Signal Box

'DOWN' TRAINS

Total Trains	from	to	Lever movements per train	Lever movements levers normal	Total lever movements
1	Down plat	LMR	2	4	4
2	Shed	LMR	12	18	36
93	Dingle	LMR	7	14	1,302
2	Herculaneum	Sands	5	10	20
2	Herculaneum	LMR	7	14	28
19	Dingle	Sands	5	10	190
6	Down plat	Shed	7	12	72
14	Down plat	Up plat	6	10	140
					Total: 1,792

'UP' TRAINS

Total Trains	from	to	Lever movements per train	Lever movements levers normal	Total lever movements
1	Up plat	Dingle	2	4	4
6	Shed	Up plat	9	12	72
20	Sands	Dingle	2	4	80
95	LMR	Dingle	4	8	760
2	LMR	Shed	8	10	20
					Total: 936

Total lever movement for 'down' trains: 1,792
Total lever movement for 'up' trains: 936

2,728

The new system was a considerable success. In 1929, for example, Liverpool produced one of its more memorable "pea-soupers", resulting in all traffic, road, rail and river, grinding to a myopic halt. All, that is, except the Overhead, whose drivers had such confidence in their signalling system (the colour lights were reputedly clearly visible at 600ft, double the safe stopping distance, whatever the weather) with its clarity of indication and its reliable train stops when all else failed, that they would happily drive where they could see virtually nothing. Any ageing Liverpudlian questioned on the Overhead will remark on its ability to run in fog, and any old driver will immediately explain that this was due to the excellence of the signals. Services occasionally ran a little late, which was probably due more to the excessive number of passengers than any other cause, but they never stopped.

This was discovered long before 1929, however, and it is scarcely surprising that the new system was extended to Seaforth Sands in 1925, and perhaps more surprising that it was not until 1945 that the mechanical signalling at Dingle at last succumbed to the march of progress.

The new system, because it worked to closer tolerances than the old, placed a greater premium on accuracy of timings, and in 1921 the Company rectified the lack of a standard time system on the line by installing Gent's Pulsynetic electric slave clocks in each station and both the signal boxes, with a master at Seaforth. Having only one master, however, would have meant an expensive job in laying the wires to the slaves beyond Stanley Dock swing bridge below the passage in order that the circuit should not be broken each time the bridge was swung off. While this happened only at night, Stanley was then a fairly busy dock, and the bridge was used quite frequently. The solution was to install a second master at Stanley to control the slaves south of that point, and this was partially under the control of the master at Seaforth Sands, being set to gain a few seconds each day. At 10.00am every day the Stanley master was held back until the Seaforth master released it, so that both clocks synchronised each day.

While all these alterations in the stock and signalling were proceeding, it should not be thought that the other aspects of the undertaking were static. During the early 1920s there was intense activity in the building of the new Gladstone Dock complex, and the Company's old carriage shed was so located as to hinder access to the Dock. In 1926 it was demolished and replaced with a new shed built on the site of the original Seaforth Sands Station, which had not really been essential since the opening of the connection to Seaforth & Litherland and the new station in 1905. The old shed had never been well equipped, or indeed laid out, for repair and maintenance work, and the new one was a very considerable improvement. It had seven roads, with a small shed for the steam locomotive built separately at the front. Of the seven roads within, the first three were much shorter than the others, but could, if necessary, each accommodate respectively, two, two and three 45ft coaches. This they were rarely required to do, as No. 1 often housed the various discarded carriage bogies and other equipment used for transport of rails and sleepers by the permanent way maintenance crew, while No. 2 contained the breakdown tool van and for a long time the remains of the stock burned out in the Dingle fire. No. 3 was the road normally used for major overhaul or rebuilding work. Roads 4, 5, 6 and 7 were each capable of housing two three-car trains, but No. 6 was 45ft shorter than the others, taking only "short" three-car trains. The reason for this deficiency was that at the far end was a well in the floor through which it was possible to lower bogies to the workshops below. Roads 4 & 5 each had an inspection pit. Plainly it was undersirable to have conductor rails in the sheds where work was proceeding, and trains were moved by means of an insulated jumper cable. Built into the side of the longitudinal sleepers used for the running rails was a 500V supply with various points at which the jumper lead could be attached, and the other end was then temporarily connected to the collector shoe of the train which was to be moved, enabling it to be driven in the normal way for so far as the lead would reach.

In marked contrast to the old shed, in which all lifting had to be done with hand tackle, the new shed was equipped with a 10ton electric crane by Herbert Morris which travelled nearly the whole length of roads 4, 5, 6 and 7. The coachbuilders, who needed to be close to the bodies on which they were working, had their benches and machinery in the north east corner of the shed, and the brake fitters and electricians were similarly provided for in the south east corner. Most other classes of work were solely or mainly undertaken in the workshops below, where a good deal of thought had gone into a layout which enabled a bogie to move from section to section with the minimum waste of time or labour. On lowering through the well into the workshops a bogie was placed over the pits and stripped, whence it went to the smith's shop where the axle box slides and any other riveted parts which needed removal were cut off. Beyond the smith's was the welding bay, where any parts that required such attention received it, and the frame then returned to the smith where the axle box slides, having been trued up, were

Below:
Colour light signal and control boxes.
C. E. Box

riveted back on. The truck was now ready for reassembly onto its wheels, which would have been either re-machined or re-tyred, then the motor was mounted on. The motor itself may have been the object of some attention, for the workshops had their own armature winding section and bearings may have been re-machined or replaced. Finally the brake gear was assembled and set up correctly. If new bearings had been installed the truck was lifted clear of the ground and the motor given a trial run to minimise the chance of a bearing heating later. While all this proceeded below, the coachbuilders were attending to the body in the shed above, and in this way it was possible for trains to be completely overhauled at the rate of about one week per coach.

Virtually none of the work mentioned above was sent out: the downstairs workshop was some 250ft long, served for all of that length by a 3ton electric crane, and within it almost every kind of repair work could be undertaken. The machine shop contained a wheel lathe, axle lathe, three smaller lathes, a planing machine, two drilling machines (one radial) a screwing machine, a grindstone and an emery wheel. These were all driven from a short lineshaft which was in turn driven by a single electric motor, with a gas engine as standby. The smithy was equipped with a small (60lb) power hammer, and the fires were electrically blown. In the brass shop were two further small lathes and a spindle drilling machine, and also a compressor, drying oven, hydraulic tyre pressing pit and the mobile welding equipment. The ground floor also accommodated the armature winding shop, and the trimmers and painters. The stores and mess room were on the ground floor, and offices for engineer, draughtsman and foreman, together with a general office were situated on a half-level in the south east corner.

Since the building of the Company's power station a great deal of progress had been made in the efficiency of generating plant, almost all of it tending to the building of ever larger power stations, and in the early twenties it was becoming apparent that, however well-run and well-equipped the Company's power station might be, it was simply not of sufficient size to produce the power required at a price which was competitive with that of public supply systems. This was not because the Company had been unwilling to attempt improvement: on the contrary a number of alterations had been made since the last major addition to capacity in 1900.

In 1907 the efficiency of the boiler house had been improved by the addition of an induced draught plant, driven at about 510rpm by a 30hp electric motor supplied by the Lancashire Dynamo Company. The capacity of the unit was sufficient to handle the gases from up to 4,500lb of coal per hour at a temperature of 500°F with a water gauge resistance of 2in at the fan inlet. The following year, the huge battery was replaced with two new ones, again by Electrical Power Storage, each having a capacity of 650amp/hours at 500V and charged from or discharging to the main bus bar. The normal charging rate for the two batteries in parallel was 520A, and the maximum permissible rate 780A. Each cell had 13 positive and 14 negative plates, 14in square,

Below:
A colour light signal and a semaphore signal at Herculaneum. *C. E. Box*

and was contained in a case of wood lined with lead measuring 16½in by 24in by 19in deep. Each battery had 248 such cells, mounted in long lines on single tier stands.

Between 1909 and 1914 a programme of dynamo replacement proceeded, as the original Elwell Parker dynamos were both showing their age and of obsolete design. The new machines were all by the Electric Construction Company, and were six-pole shunt-wound, with interpoles, rated at 250kW. The first pair was installed in 1909, and produced its 500A at 500V output at a speed of 400rpm, while the further pairs, installed in 1911 and 1914 produced the same output at 380rpm. All were, like their predecessors, rope driven. The big British Shuckert generator (No. 7) which was direct coupled to the Browett, Lindley engine had been replaced at an unknown date prior to 1909 with an 850kW 12-pole shunt-wound unit by Dick, Kerr which produced 1,700A at 500V. No further alterations or additions were made to the main generating plant, but a number of changes took place in other areas. The original main board had been replaced in 1896 when the plant was enlarged to supply the Southern Extension, and the various alterations made would plainly require a new board at some stage. One further group of changes took place before the new board was installed, when in 1912, new control equipment for the batteries was supplied by the Electrical Power Storage Company. In order to maintain as steady a load as possible on the main generators, it was desirable to have an automatic and responsive arrangement for charging or discharging the batteries according to the varying load on the line. This began with an ENTZ reversible rotary positive booster whose output was automatically switched from the storage batteries to the bus bars or vice-versa, as required. When an exceptionally heavy demand for traction current arose a solenoid became strongly energised and made the circuit through the discharge side of a carbon regulator, which then passed from the batteries to the booster as much power as was needed. Should the load fall suddenly the solenoid would be partially released, making the circuit through the charge side of the regulator to the batteries, thus taking up any surplus current not required for traction and storing it. This was a very much more sensitive arrangement than relying on the rather ponderous governors of the main engines, and also allowed battery charging to be carried out while there was a load on the line, which had not previously been possible. The booster was capable of passing a normal rate of charge to the batteries of 260A, with a maximum rate of charge of 390A. It was also capable of handling a peak load for a brief period of about ten seconds, of 2000A, to cover starting surges on the line. The new main board followed in 1917, being designed and supplied by British Thomson-Houston of Rugby, and installed by the LORs own staff. It was situated on the north side of the main generating room with the Tramway board adjoining it on the west side and the booster board on the east side. It was an impressive piece of equipment, 7ft 6in high and 35ft 5in long, and with the exception of the signalling supply equipment mentioned above was the last new equipment installed in the generating station.

The generating station had been, in many respects, the pride of the company. In the best traditions of stationary steam engineering, it had always been a highly polished temple to the God of Steam and of course it had the immense attraction, totally absent in turbo-alternator plant, of large shiny pieces of metal moving around in an eminently comprehensible manner and slowly enough to be seen and admired. Unfortunately, no amount of this kind of aesthetic appeal could alter the fact that the railway only required about 4 million to 5 million units per year, and that it was not economic to run such a small station. A number of enquiries were made about the supply of power from outside sources, but it was not until 1927 that an agreement was reached with Liverpool Corporation for power from their system. The last full year's working of the Company's station showed a cost of 1.09d per unit, while the first complete year of working on the Corporation supply showed a reduction to 0.884d. To some degree this was accounted for by a reduction in the price of coal, but the savings continued: by 1932 the cost was down to 0.786d, a reduction of some 28%.

The power station was closed on 26 June 1927: some of the equipment was sold for re-use and some broken up and sold for scrap. The power house and the chimney were demolished.

While the traction supply could be drawn directly from the Corporation system, the 600V ac supply for the signalling system could not, and to meet this requirement a small new building, known as Signal House was erected half-way down the incline just to the North of Nelson station, on the east side of the up line. Almost

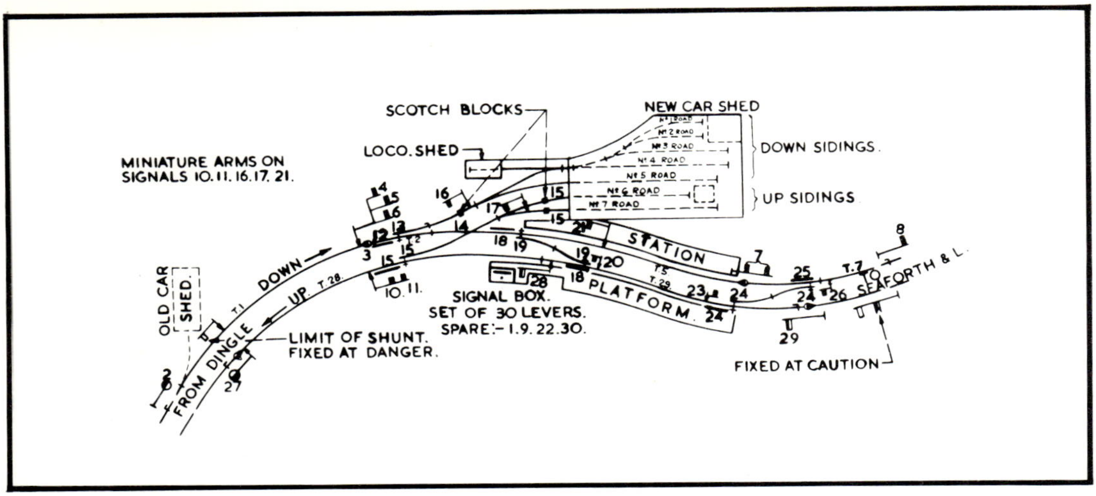

Above:
LOR 1926. Signal box 'A' at Seaforth Sands station and new carriage shed. Not to scale.

Above right:
The signals and the overlapping.

opposite the former site of the power station. The Corporation supply was taken from their Paradise Street sub-station to Custom House Station, where there was a small distribution board, and thence by a special cable to Signal House. This was, of course, a dc supply at the normal 500V-525V pressure. In the event of failure on this supply, a standby supply could be taken from the conductor rail immediately outside Signal House. Inside the building were the motor alternators to provide the ac supply with their switchboard together with staff accommodation and other necessary offices.

In 30 Mr Grundy, the General Manager left the Company, and Mr George Hughes was appointed Acting General Manager. Mr Hughes had been with the LOR from the start, beginning as a relief clerk in the Head Office in 1893 and working his way through various appointments in different departments until he became Assistant Manager, which position he held until appointment as Acting General Manager. Unhappily, like the majority of the senior officers of the Company, he died at the early age of 58, on 16 February 1933.

Wilfred Box, the Author's father, had been Chief Engineer since the retirement of Mr Neachell, and was now appointed General Manager, thus re-uniting the two sides of what had always, until 1926, been one post. Mr Box hailed from Twickenham, where he was born in 1878 and educated at King's College, Twickenham, later at Mercers School. His technical training was at the City and Guilds of London Institute and at King's College, London. After the then usual practice he went to serve an apprenticeship to learn the practical side of engineering, for in those unenlightened days it had yet to be realised that management was an abstract skill quite unrelated to the activity being managed. Completing his time with firms in Southwark and later Nottingham, he joined the engineering staff of the Waterloo and City Railway at the time of its opening in 1898, and later became shift engineer for the line. In 1901 he went to the English Electric Manufacturing Company, which was taken over in 1903 by Dick, Kerr of Preston. There followed a period in which he acted as Resident Engineer on a number of major projects undertaken by Dick, Kerr. In 1901 he was engaged on tramway generating stations for the Portsmouth and Great Grimsby systems, and the following year he made his first acquaintance with the LOR, being placed in charge of the conversion of the trains used for the accelerated service. In 1903 he worked on the generating and sub-station plant of the London County Council Tramways and the following year saw him in Singapore, where he remained for three years, working on the tramway system there before going on in 1907 to a similar contract in Calcutta. Returning to Britain in 1907, he worked on the construction of the British Aluminium Company's hydro-electric

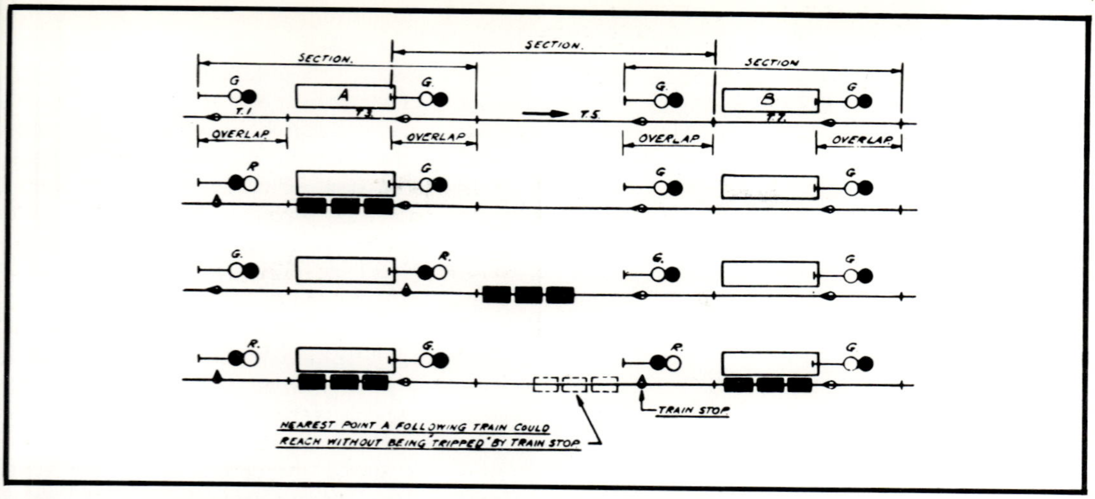

scheme at Kinlochleven, his last contract for Dick, Kerr. In 1911 he was appointed Assistant Engineer to the LOR, who must have been well pleased to find a man with such wide experience in both electric generation and traction. He was an Associate Member of the Institute of Mechanical Engineers (elected 1903) and also a member of the Liverpool Engineering Society, Fellow of the Permanent Way Institution and Associate Member of the Institution of Railway Signal Engineers.

The repeated war damage to the railway described in Chapter 9 and indeed the repeated disruption of his own office, put a great deal of strain on him, and he was particularly hard hit by the loss of his Carriage Shed Superintendent, Edward Boakes, of whom he held a very high opinion, as a result of enemy action on 1 June 1941. Suffering from failing health, he had to retire on 31 March 1943, and moved to Bournemouth, where he died later the same year, aged 65.

His successor, H. Maxwell Rostron, was born in Waterloo on 31 December 1900 and educated successively at Merchant Taylors School, Bootle Technical School, and the Central Technical School, Liverpool. His family was very well known on Merseyside, for his father was Captain Sir Arthur Rostron, who was in command of the Cunarder *Carpathia* when she made her desperate dash to pick up survivors of the *Titanic*. He and his crew were successful in saving 706 lives, having worked up their ship to a speed well in excess of its design maximum, and maintained that speed for several hours. He later became Captain of what was perhaps Liverpool's most famous ocean greyhound, *Mauretania*, a command he held from 1915 until 1926, when he was appointed Commodore of the Cunard Fleet and Captain of *QSS Berengaria*. That his son should become General Manager and Engineer of the LOR might be seen as symbolising that essential interaction between shipping and rail transport which had first led Sir William Forwood to get the railway, if the reader will pardon the expression, off the ground.

The new General Manager had, however, been exiled from Merseyside for some time, for after serving his apprenticeship with James Scott Ltd, electrical and mechanical engineers in Bootle, he left at the age of 22 (though not before he had risen to being in charge of a department) and joined the staff at the Dick, Kerr Works, which was by then part of English Electric Co, in the traction test department. In 1925 he moved on, to Pirelli-General Cable Works Ltd, of Southampton as first Assistant Engineer for outside contracts, after which he returned home to Liverpool for a while as District Engineer and Representative. He then moved to the Sales Department at Southampton, and finally to the works at Eastleigh. During his time with Pirelli-General he was involved in some very large cabling contracts, including that for the electrification of parts of the Southern Railway. On his return to Liverpool he became involved in many local activities, beginning with the Home Guard, in which he held a commission, and he also became one of the first student members of the Liverpool branch of the Institution of Electrical Engineers, of which be became as Associate and was transferred to Membership in

1950. He was also a member of the Liverpool Engineering Society and of the Liverpool Amateur Photographic Association. Fellowship of the Permanent Way Institution and Membership of the Institution of Mechanical Engineers complete an impressive list of professional activities and qualifications.

On taking up his post he was faced immediately with the appalling task which had forced Mr Box to retire, namely keeping the railway working under war conditions, and the successful achievement of this labour is described in Chapter 9. No less demanding, however, was the task of taking the little railway forward into a post-war world on a basis of 50 year old stock and a structure which was feeling its age. There could be no doubt that changes would be necessary, of which perhaps the most obvious one was probably unimportant, but merely symbolic. In August 1947 a Ruston & Hornsby diesel locomotive was purchased, foreshadowing the end of the line for the veteran *Lively Polly*. The new locomotive was a four-wheeler, 17ft 8in overall length and 7ft 5in at its widest point with an overall height of 10ft 0⅜in. The wheels were of 2ft 6in diameter, on a wheelbase of 5ft 2¾in between centres. A Ruston four-stroke diesel engine of the four cylinder VRO class provided 44bhp at 1000rpm, and the drive passed through a gearbox giving three forward ratios and three reverse before arriving at the axles via a pair of chains. Data for the different gear ratios were as follows:

Gear	Speed range mph	Drawbar pull in lb	Maximum tons hauled on the straight: Level	1 in 200	1 in 100	1 in 80	1 in 50	1 in 30	1 in 20
1	2 to 4	3,270	163	102	73	64	45	29	18½
2	3.1 to 6.2	2,060	137	75	51	43	29	17	9½
3	4.75 to 9.5	1,290	86	46	30	25	16	8	3½

Below:
The steam loco *Polly* undergoing a heavy overhaul at Seaforth. *C. E. Box*

Below right:
The old and the new. *Polly* and the new diesel shunter together at Seaforth in 1948.
C. E. Box

The diesel locomotive had, inevitably, a great advantage over steam for the Company's purpose in that it was always ready for action without having to wait for steam to be raised. Nevertheless, it seems to have failed to generate sufficient affection for anyone to trouble to give it a name. The displaced *Lively Polly* was sold early in January 1948 and transported to Wrexham, where she was overhauled by Cudworth & Johnson, and in June the following year she was delivered to the Rea Coal Wharf, which operated on the site of the old Monk's Ferry Station of the Chester and Birkenhead Railway, close to Woodside. The wharf was mainly used for bunkering tugs, and with the decline of coal firing the days of the wharf had to be numbered. It finally closed in 1961, and on 23 August that year the Central Wagon Company of Ince (near Wigan) began work on breaking up *Lively Polly,* after a working life of 68 years.

Of greater real consequence was the decision taken in 1944 to begin a programme of train modernisation which would, for the first time, amount to much more than re-equipment. A complete change in appearance was sought, in order to give the LOR a more up-to-date image – an image which one must admit the old stock most conspicuously lacked, and soon afterwards work began on producing a prototype modernised coach. This was a complete re-bodying job, but the bogies were the originals, suitably overhauled. The chosen guinea pig was motor No. 29, and in February 1945 it was put in service, resplendent in composite aluminium panelling below window level, with a new driver's compartment layout, a tidied-up roofline and improved interior lighting. Lest the passengers should find it all too strange and new, the original (and highly uncomfortable) slatted wooden seats still lurked within. The second modernised coach, No 30 emerged in February the following year, and went a good deal further in its changes, with a completely aluminium-panelled exterior and electro-pneumatic sliding doors operated by the guard. Streamlined ventilators were fitted to the roof, while inside a new modern-styled lighting system and tubular framed seats with leather upholstery appeared. In 1947 the first complete modernised train went into service, made up of coaches No. 14-7-30. It embodied all the features which had appeared on No. 30 and also introduced the new-style first class accommodation, which had handsome timber framed seating upholstered in moquette. All interiors were panelled in matched-veneer plywood, and all had stainless steel interior fittings. A second modernised train was completed later the same year, No. 15-12-16,

which was basically similar to No. 14-7-30, but exhibited some variations, including larger windows, different door spacings and an altered seating layout.

Below:
An official LOR postcard showing the construction of the new Gladstone Dock, to be the largest graving dock in the world – a unique view being obtained only from LOR trains.

Whilst the production of the modernised stock had been successful, there were two obvious problems, namely that the mechanical parts were very old and that a prolonged rebuilding programme would place a great strain on the workshop facilities of a small company. It was therefore decided to seek a quotation for the construction of entirely new three-car trains of pressed aluminium construction, embodying the successful features already found on the two rebuilt trains. The quotation was for a maximum price of £22,000 per train, on condition that a minimum of five trains was ordered, which meant a minimum outlay of £110,000. This was

more than the Company was able to afford, and rebuilding therefore proceeded in the Seaforth Sands Carriage Shed, carried out by the Company's own staff. New traction motors and control gear were gradually fitted to virtually all of the stock, and trains with the new bodywork were placed in service at the rate of one per year from 1950 until 1955, in the following order: Nos 5-15-11, 8-14-24, 1-13-22, 18-5-29, 26-9-28, 10-4-12. Prior to this, the original modernised train, 14-7-30 had been the new train of 1949, having been altered to make its windows match all the others, but it could always be "spotted" by the different spacing of its doors. The later six trains were all identical except in a few details. Two of the motor coaches, Nos 1 and 22 were fitted with disc wheels, instead of the spoked ones used on all previous stock and the modernised trailer cars were fitted with an interior lining of plastic instead of plywood. This was of mahogany colour in the first four, and walnut colour in the later ones.

Successive alterations to stock had given rise to a very wide variation in seating capacities between different trains, the lowest being a mere 120 and the largest 242. Details of the capacities as at the beginning of 1956 are shown in the appendix.

9. In adversity

An undertaking as novel as the LOR might well have been expected to suffer a crop of minor accidents in its early years, especially since it had such an untried signalling system. In fact the railway had a completely accident-free record for the first few years of operation, an achievement which was quite remarkable. Unfortunately, when the first accident came, although not the result of a collision, it was a serious one, resulting in six deaths.

At 5pm on 23 December 1901 train No. 32-5-35 left Seaforth Sands Station. It was one of the heaviest trains of the day, carrying large numbers of homeward workers from the docks and it left in thoroughly evil weather, with heavy rain driven by a gale-force wind. Labouring against load and weather, the train eventually arrived at Herculaneum 8min late, by which time the majority of its passengers had alighted. It was equipped with two direct-drive 70hp motors, one on the leading axle of the train and the other at the extreme rear; neither motor was iron cased, and a strong smell due to overheating was noticed. The train left Herculaneum with 29 passengers still aboard, rounded the curve, crossed the bridge, and made its fatal way into the tunnel. The signalman on duty in the Dingle box had set the road for the down platform and pulled off the home signal, so the train could run straight in. From his box he could see the train approaching, apparently normally, until it suddenly came to a stand about 80yds short of the platform.

The driver found his automatic circuit breaker had opened, but did not appreciate that this was because the rear motor had failed completely. With only 80yds to go, he took what may have seemed a permissible risk, and re-set the breaker. The result was an intense arc which set fire to the rear of the train, and the driver, seeing this, switched out. Despite the fact that the flare-up had been extremely violent, almost extinguishing the station lights, he now made an incomprehensible decision. Knowing that the rear motor was defective, and very seriously so, he did not disconnect it, which he could and should easily have done from his cab, but again threw the breaker in. The result was another large flare-up, and it is recorded that at this point the guard shouted from the rear of the train: "You will have us burnt up if you go on like this". In this he was proved right. The driver decided that if the train were relieved of the load of the curve and entrance points it might yet limp into the platform, and accordingly hailed the signalman, asking him to set the road for the up line, giving a straight approach. This the signalman did, but instead of the crippled train creeping in, it remained still, a third flare-up at the rear revealing yet a third connection of the failed motor by the driver. By this time the train was well alight; the heavy wind conditions above provided considerable draughts which caused the flames to pass from coach to coach.

Because the track was still live, the driver and guard at first asked the passengers to remain in the burning train, and attempted to fight the fire. These attempts were totally ineffectual, and eventually the passengers alighted, walked to the station and made their way home. Two only remained to enjoy the spectacle; it was their last earthly pleasure. The guard now hailed the signalman to ask him to call the generating station to ask them to cut off the current, but the message was in fact passed by the station foreman, who overheard the request and made the call from the platform telephone. This apparently prudent move, which would enable the hydrants on the platform to be used in safety actually served to make the situation worse, as it plunged the entire station into darkness, making for total confusion and creating great difficulties for those still attempting to make their escape.

By now the fire was totally beyond control, with huge quantities of pungent smoke and fumes rising from the burning train; an evil brew made up from burning wood, upholstery, insulation materials and paint. In the short tunnel beyond the platforms there was an air shaft, which, as the heat and draught increased began to act as a chimney, with the result that the flames were drawn from the burning train along the tunnel like the flue gases of some huge boiler. In No. 2 siding, some 8 yards from the train a stack of stored sleepers ignited, followed by the signal box 55yds distant, the platform (80yds) and finally a spare train in No. 4 Siding which was no less than 155yds away. The smoke and fumes grew denser all the time, until a point was inevitably reached where no living thing could survive.

While all this was unfolding below ground, the only chance of rescue lay in the Fire Brigade above. No brigade in the country at that date had a motor appliance, so while passengers and staff fought for their lives firemen were harnessing horses and lighting the fires on the steam pumps. One can picture that little harbinger of doom, the Brigade Dog, racing to Dingle with horses at a gallop behind, while below ground life ebbed away. The Brigade did not manage to arrive until 30min after the fire began, by which time the upward rush of smoke, fumes and hot gases was so violent that they were unable to descend far enough to reach to seat of the fire.

The last to escape from the inferno were the signalman, his train booking boy, and a passenger. Each of these lost consciousness just before or just after reaching safety in the booking hall, so that no very clear explanation of exactly how they escaped was obtainable. The boy had shown great courage and initiative in employing his detailed knowledge of the station to guide out a number of passengers after the lights went out, most probably saving them from the fate of the six who remained. Of those, four were employees of the railway, who should have been able to find their way out. Presumably the smoke and fumes, which fouled the air from the top of the tunnel downwards, cut off their escape before they realised the immediacy of their predicament in getting upwards through what must have been an impenetrable barrier of hot and poisonous gas. The driver was found by the front of his train. His guard and car cleaner lay at the approach end of the platform, near the signal box. The station foreman and the two curious passengers had attempted to escape to the shaft of the end tunnel, only to succumb to the chimney effect there. Curiously no-one appears to have attempted escape by heading towards Herculaneum.

After the fire, it was discovered that nothing remained of the platform or any other combustible structure of the station. The two trains were completely burned out, and a third which had been standing in siding No. 3 was badly scorched. The station could not be reopened until early in 1903, non-combustible materials having been extensively employed in the new construction work. No. 2 siding was not rebuilt, but otherwise the station was reinstated much as it had been before the worst disaster to befall the railway in its entire history.

The first working accident on the line occurred on 19 December 1908, when a train ran into the buffer stops at Seaforth Sands Station, but this was of very little consequence: far more serious were two accidents in 1919, both occurring in fog. On 13 January the 7.17 train from Dingle, (Nos 2-15) ran into Brocklebank Station on the normal down line, and collided with the rear of the 7.13 (39-3-40) which was standing there.

Above:

Posters being displayed at the beginning of the War and possibly assisting with the 'Holidays at Home' scheme. *George Cohen 600 Group*

Within a month an almost carbon copy accident occurred at Clarence down platform, when the 7.29 from Dingle collided with the rear of the 7.33. While these accidents could scarcely be considered as disasters, they did reveal an obvious and intolerable defect in the signalling system as originally installed, and an entirely new system was devised and installed to prevent any repetition.

When war broke out in 1939 it was fairly clear that, sooner or later, Liverpool would become, as she had been in the First World War, a crucial centre of North Atlantic convoy operations, and thus that she would be a priority target for the new-style warfare of heavy aerial bombardment. The LOR was in one of the most vulnerable positions in the City, close to all of the Docks and a moderately desirable target in itself. The 'Phoney War' ended for the railway at 11.40pm on 17 August 1940, when a bomb fell on the west side of the structure, south of Brunswick Station, but did very little damage, blowing away a handrail and severing two electric cables. On 31 August the first serious damage was suffered, when a bomb fell at 11.00pm on the structure between James Street and Custom House Stations near to the middle of a span, virtually cutting through a main girder and another hit one of the supports of the James Street bow girder bridge. This latter added insult to injury by shattering the windows of the Company offices at 31 James Street. The following morning a few hours' work sufficed to get trains running again from Seaforth to Pier Head and from Dingle to Brunswick, with a special Corporation bus service providing the link. No trains were able to work right through until November, for the damage was soon compounded in other places.

On the evening of Thursday 26 September a heavier air raid caused several difficulties: at Wapping part of a warehouse collapsed onto the structure, buckling the main girders of a 50ft span, while at Brunswick no less than six spans were buckled by the heat generated when about 50 loaded wagons standing in sidings in the Dock Estate were burned. In this area fires were still being fought three days after the raid. At Toxteth a bomb landing near one of the main columns blew it completely to pieces. Two trains stabled in Herculaneum carriage shed were moved into the tunnel until services could be resumed, to protect them from gratuitous damage. In fact, however, a short period of respite followed, for no damage was suffered again until 7.00pm on 11 October, when an incendiary scorched signal cables on the bow girder bridge at Gladstone Dock, but operation was not affected. Another fell through the roof of the Carriage Shed roof at Seaforth, but did little damage, while a third hit Gladstone Dock Station but this also was fairly promptly extinguished with little damage. The Mersey Tunnel Ventilator at Pier Head was hit, causing large amounts of debris to fall on the structure, but it proved able to sustain the weight. A similar misfortune befell the structure near Wapping on 28 October, when about 50ton of rubble fell from a warehouse, but again the structure held. Other high explosive bombs dropped in the same raid fell near the railway, but only one did any damage, blowing up a staircase at Wapping Station. No further raids affected the railway before 25 November, when repairs were sufficiently far advanced for through trains to work again, and the next hits were not sustained until 20 December, when the attack was largely switched from the South to the North Docks. Damage to the structure meant that only a fragmentary service was possible, with normal working from Seaforth Sands to Alexandra, single line working from Alexandra to Brocklebank, double line working from Clarence to Pier Head, buses covering all the gaps. The bombing also caused inconvenience by breaking the telephone link between the LOR and the General Manager's home at Great Crosby. The raids continued for two further nights, with some daytime bombing as well. The most serious damage was at Canada Dock station, where a platform was completely shattered, and two 50ft spans just to the south collapsed, completely blocking the Dock Railway. Minor damage occurred to the structure at Huskisson, and some handrails were blown away at Seaforth Sands. Makeshift services were further curtailed by the presence of a number of time bombs, one under the down road between Seaforth & Litherland and Seaforth Sands, and others between Pier Head and Huskisson. Until 23 December, when the first of these was successfully de-fused, the service was double line between Seaforth LMS and Seaforth Sands, thence single line to Brocklebank on the down road. Single down line working resumed between Huskisson and Pierhead, and again buses provided cover between Brocklebank and Huskisson and from Pier Head to Dingle.

Another period of respite followed, with rapid repair work in progress, which remained undisturbed from the air until March. Repairs made to the structure along the South Docks were tested from Toxteth to Brunswick on 6 February, and from Brunswick to Pier Head the following day, so that regular through traffic from Pier Head to Dingle was able to resume on 9 February. Exactly a month later, two 3-car trains were coupled together and left the carriage sheds at 7.35am to make the first through test since the December raids. The train ran on the down line from Seaforth to Huskisson, crossing to the up line from Huskisson to Herculaneum, where they were heavily loaded with brake blocks, sand, anything heavy which came to hand, and despatched to test the rebuilt structure between Canada and Huskisson. The test was satisfactory, but bore little fruit, for a heavy raid on the night of Wednesday 12 March destroyed both roads at the foot of the incline at Nelson Dock and damaged the up platform at Princes so extensively that it was unsafe to use. The repair gangs may have gained some sort of consolation that night from the fact that a tremendous anti-aircraft barrage, supplemented by the long range fire of the main armaments of warships in the river, succeeded in bringing down seven of the raiders, a new nocturnal shooting record. The damage at Nelson was repaired by 27 March, when a through service was again available right from Seaforth to Dingle for the first time since December. Relative peace reigned again until the start of the May Blitz, which lasted from Friday, 2 May for almost exactly a week.

This was a systematic attempt to close the Port of Liverpool from the air, but here as elsewhere, the Luftwaffe had overestimated its capabilities and underestimated the determination of the civilian population to carry on business as normal. They had also underestimated the likely rate of aircraft loss, with the result that the May Blitz was virtually the end of strategic bombing over Merseyside. From the railway's point of view most of the damage occurred in the early stages, with six spans destroyed on the first night, three (Nos 379-381) at James Street and three (442-444) at Wapping. James Street Station was completely wrecked and the Company's office was again damaged, this time so seriously shaken as to be structurally unsafe. A train in Pier Head Station was commandeered by the General Manager as a temporary Head Office, and the following night the James Street Office was again hit, this time being almost totally destroyed, its final demise coming on Sunday night, when the remains were burned to the ground. Meanwhile, on Saturday night two spans at Canada Dock, (Nos 176 and 201) had been destroyed. In Huskisson No. 2 Branch Dock one of the Luftwaffe's luckiest hits caused the explosion of the Brocklebank liner Malakand, laden with over 1,000ton of munitions. The ship, dock and surrounding buildings were so severely damaged that no attempt was made to effect repairs, and the branch was eventually filled in. The railway structure was badly shaken by this colossal blast and rendered unsafe. Extensive fires, which could be seen over 40 miles away in North Wales, raged along the Dock Road, with the result that the temporary services on isolated sections which had been running after Friday's raids had to be discontinued. Further difficulties were caused by delayed action bombs strewn about the area.

On Sunday the main weight of the assault was transferred to Belfast, but some bombs were dropped, without any additional damage to the railway, and this sporadic raiding continued on Monday and Tuesday, with heavy attacks being reserved for Barrow and the Clyde. On Tuesday night the General Manager could have been forgiven for imagining that he had become a priority target, for his new temporary offices in Tower Building had their windows blown in, a further raid the following night rendering the building unsafe, with the result that he once again had to operate from a train, this time in Seaforth Sands Carriage Shed. The same night two spans at Canada Dock (Nos 180 & 181) were destroyed, and again huge fires burned in the city. Heavy raids with parachute mines were made over working class residential areas, but the railway escaped comparatively lightly, and the two spans at Canada proved to be the last significant damage it was to suffer. Sporadic raiding continued, but the repair gangs were once again able to start making good the damage, which they did so effectively that a limited service was able to commence running between Seaforth Sands and Alexandra and from Huskisson to Dingle by Monday 19 May. The same day the General Manager's office was again moved, this time to rooms on the fifth and seventh floors of North House in North John Street, made available by Alderman (later Sir Alfred) Shennan, where it was able to remain undisturbed until March 1947.

Work on the structure continued unabated, with attention now turned to the sections where

Right:
Serious bomb damage occurred near Canada station on the night of 20/21 December 1940. This photograph shows the extent of the damage to the structure and it was not until 3 September 1941 that the line was re-opened at this point. *Stewart Bale Ltd*

the really serious damage had occurred. Repairs to, and in some parts complete rebuilding of, the structure occupied surprisingly short time when one considers the difficulties faced, and on Monday 1 September 1941 the section from Canada to Pier Head was tested, found satisfactory and opened to traffic two days later. Testing of the Pier Head to Wapping section was carried out on 29 October and on Saturday 1 November the railway was again opened to traffic from end to end, remaining so for the rest of the war. Absolute determination that the Railway should remain open so far as imaginably possible had prevailed, and it was left to a more destructive set of circumstances than mere war to close it.

With the end of the war the railway continued without further disaster until 4 February 1956, when, at 3.45am a Bootle Police constable passing on his beat found Seaforth Sands Station ablaze and raised the alarm. A rapid turn out by the Fire Brigade saw several major appliances on the scene, reinforcements soon bringing the total to eight, with 50 firemen involved. The fire was a serious one; two trains were normally left standing in the station overnight, ready to operate the first service of the morning, and these as well as the station were burning furiously, with flames leaping 20ft above the roof, but within 45min the Brigade had it under control. An unfortunate minor side effect was that on a bitterly cold night the water which spread across roads and pavements from their efforts rapidly froze into a treacherous sheet of ice to the discomfiture of passers-by, necessitating hasty distribution of sand and salt.

Passengers arriving early that morning found chalked notices at the street-level booking office informing them that there was no service from that station, though trains ran normally between Alexandra and Dingle. Inside the damage was being assessed and the cause investigated. The up platform of the station was very seriously damaged, while of the two trains two cars survived slightly damaged. The coaches there had been Nos 2-6-9 at the up platform and Nos 10-4-12 at the down: of these Nos 2, 6, 4 and 12 were total wrecks. The three-car trains at that time were valued at about £10,000 each, and the total damage due to the fire was estimated at £30,000. The cause was fairly clearly arson. A number of serious fires, without obvious accidental cause, had broken out in the Seaforth area about that time and in this case there was a watchman in the workshops below who had carried out his regular round of inspection only 45min before the discovery of the fire and had found everything in order. The fire was found to have originated in the ladies' waiting room, where the remains of a motor tyre and of an upholstered seat removed from one of the trains were found. Officers of the CID were called in, and were assisted by fire experts from the Home Office Forensic Laboratory at Preston, but the culprit was never discovered.

With the same determination to keep running which had existed during the war, the railway set about getting back to normal. The signal box at

Alexandra was opened to work the cross over road there, enabling a full service to be run from there until Seaforth Sands could be reopened, which was achieved in only two days. An interesting operational problem was posed by the two remaining operable coaches, No. 9 (one of the original batch) and No. 10 which was one of the latest modernised stock. They had survived because they were each at the north end of their respective trains, which meant that they could not be used as a two-car train unless one of them was turned, for they were both facing the same way.

On Sunday 19 February, therefore, Motor Coach No. 9 departed on its unusual solo run, leaving Seaforth at 9.45am and proceeding to Southport, Chapel Street, where it was scheduled to arrive at 10.25am running into platform 3. Freshfield signal box was reached at 10.09am, but 198yds beyond the box stood the down advance starter for Freshfield station, which was at danger, and remained so for about two minutes. This put No. 9 behind its booked time, and Mr S. W. E. Jones (LOR Rolling Stock Superintendent) who was in charge of the manoeuvre, instructed his driver to drive in parallel. The speeds attained in first and last parallel notches were probably of the order of 30 and 38 mph respectively, and Southport was reached at 10.23, two minutes ahead of the booked time. The distance from Freshfield down advance starter to Southport Station box was 6 miles 351yds, and was covered in twelve minutes, an average speed, start to stop, of very nearly 30mph. At 10.35am the coach pulled out of platform 3, and ran round the triangle just outside the station, leaving St. Luke's at 10.45am, arriving at Southport South at 10.50am, leaving at 11.05am. Now facing in the correct direction, No. 9 headed for Seaforth and Litherland, where she was scheduled to arrive at 11.46am and leave at 11.48am, arriving at Seaforth South at 11.50am. It might have been expected that trouble would be encountered with power collection, as No. 9 had only two collector shoes, one on each side at the front, but in the event she had no difficulty in crossing the gaps in the conductor rails at points or level crossings, and the trip was successfully accomplished.

10. The End of the Line

The first suggestions of possible serious trouble for the railway had come as early as 1933, when quite extensive repair work had been necessary on the structure. It had proved impossible over the years completely to eliminate movement between the longitudinal sleepers and the arched deckplates, which came about as a result of thermal expansion and contraction of structure, sleepers and rails and was exacerbated by the braking, acceleration and centrifugal loads imposed by the trains. Over the 40 years the line had been in service the sleepers had with the aid of damp, detached scale and windborne grit, worn their way right through the arch of the plates in many places. This had been dealt with by riveting patches of 5/16in plate, curved to match the arched section, over the holes. Many tons of dirt were removed from the drainage channels, but the harm done by the damp which had thus been retained was not completely eliminated.

By 1954 the condition of the structure was again the cause of serious concern, with maintenance costs mounting. This concern was heightened by the fact that the number of passengers carried was showing a slight decline, which, although far from disastrous, would diminish the Company's ability to meet those rising costs.

It was decided by the Board that the best course of action would be to engage an independent firm of consultants to examine the whole of the structure and prepare a comprehensive report thereon. The report was commissioned in 1954, and received in January the following year. It did not make cheerful reading, for it confirmed the fears of the Board that a large part of the structure was in fairly imminent need of renewal. In particular it was going to be necessary to renew the decking, a task which was said to be needful of undertaking within five years.

The structure of the railway was subject to considerable strains from the passage on trains, most particularly from the effects of centrifugal force upon the trains at curves, and it was comparatively lightly built for the loads involved, which meant that it had to be maintained in a near optimal condition. In retrospect it is fairly clear that this would not be possible for a wrought iron structure given the conditions in which it had to exist. Not only did it have to face Liverpool's distinctive brand of horizontal rain, together with a good deal of industrial atmospheric pollution and a certain amount of wind-borne salt spray from the river, it also had the Dock Railway underneath it. The Dock Board's locomotives were equipped with a smoke deflector plate mounted on a pivot in a boss on the smokebox side which was supposed to be swung over the chimney top when operating under the Overhead structure to prevent the underside of the decking being exposed to the full effects of the blast. These little locomotives frequently pulled very heavy loads, involving labouring in full gear, and the deflector plate did absolutely nothing to help the steaming of the boiler, with the result that its use was frequently forgotten, in rather the same way that large holes burned through the middle of the spark arrestors often seem to have escaped the eagle eyes of the footplate crews. The result was a good deal of evil sulphurous condensation on the underside of the decking, eating its way upwards to join the rust working its way down from water trapped in the corrugations of the deck. The deck had been a very clever structure in terms of its solution of a number of problems in the original building, but the shape of the joints between the plates taken in conjunction with the requirement that it be waterproof meant that if the rainwater disposal was anything less than perfect corrosion along the line of rivets must inevitably result sooner or later.

The estimated cost of the repairs thus rendered necessary was in excess of £2 million, which for a company with gross annual receipts in the order of £150,000 and a total issued capital of £827,500 was totally beyond the bounds of possibility, either from existing resources or from the issue of new shares or debenture stock. The Directors were therefore of the opinion that the only sensible course of action, in the interests of all classes of shareholders, was to cut the anticipated losses by closing the railway before such huge expenditure was necessary. The

Above :
A few days before closure with one of the modernised trains.

Below:
Monday 31 December 1956 and a Liverpool Corporation bus on their new route 1 replaces the trains and waits at Seaforth terminus, for the journey to Dingle. *Ian Allan Library*

opinion of Counsel was therefore sought as to the legal mechanisms for closure, and the advice received was to the effect that a private bill authorising closure should be placed before Parliament in November 1955. If the Bill were free of serious objection it could receive the Royal Assent and become effective by July the following year. On the basis of this advice, the shareholders at their half-yearly general meeting, held on 25 July 1955 decided that they should voluntarily close the railway. Even this was not a course of action entirely free of difficulties, for there were 230 employees to be compensated for the loss of their jobs, which would cost up to £50,000. A more serious difficulty from the shareholders point of view was that the Company was responsible for the complete demolition and removal of the structure, an operation which would not have been particularly simple even without the necessity of avoiding the obstruction of traffic along the Dock Road, through the numerous dock gateways under or near the structure and along the main line of the Dock Railway. It was in fact such a complicated demolition job that, despite the considerable tonnage of scrap metal in the structure, it might end up with a net loss to shareholders: they would be at the mercy of short term fluctuations in the price of scrap. To make matters worse, the job would also be a long and slow one, so that the finalisation of the Company's finances would most likely take some considerable time.

The report for the final year's working gave the following figures.

Nominal capital authorised and created by the company:	
	£
Shares and stocks, LOR Co Act, 1888	450,000
Shares and stocks, LOR Co Act, 1892	120,000
Shares and stocks, LOR Co Act, 1899	50,000
Shares and stocks, LOR Co Act, 1900	60,000
	£680,000

Share capital isssued:	
	£
12,000 Preference Shares (1892 issue) of £10 each	120,000
3,862 Preference Shares (1900 issue) of £10 each	38,620
50,000 Ordinary Shares of £10 each	500,000
	£658,620

Capital raised by the issue of 4 per cent Debenture Stock, £168,880.

	1956	1955
	£	£
Railway – Gross receipts	159,877	161,971
Expenditure	140,828	138,569
Net Receipts	19,049	23,402

Expenditure in respect of railway working:	1956	1955
	£	£
A – Maintenance of way and works	15,137	18,570
B – Maintenance of rolling stock	16,061	17,012
C – Locomotive running expenses	24,623	23,553
D – Traffic expenses	71,885	64,711

Abstract A (part) – Maintenance of way and works:	1956	1955
Maintenance of roads, bridges, tunnels and other	£	£
works	727	668
Maintenance of structure	2,338	4,636
Maintenance of permanent way materials	1,578	2,325
Maintenance of signalling	2,104	2,040
Maintenance of telegraphs	198	148
Maintenance of electric track equipment	716	2,112
Maintenance of stations, depots and offices	1,463	1,874

Abstract B (part) – Maintenance of rolling stock:		
	1956	1955
	£	£
Electric motor coaches:		
Repairs and partial renewals	12,974	12,977
Trailer Coaches:		
Repairs and partial renewals	2,135	3,129

Abstract C (part) – Locomotive Running Expenses:		
	1956	1955
	£	£
Electric train working:		
Wages of motormen	13,820	12,775
Electric current	10,025	10,165
Lubricants	180	174

Abstract D (part) – Traffic Expenses:		
	1856	1955
	£	£
Superintendence salaries and wages	1,643	1,582
Inspectors and clerks	28,277	25,957
Signalmen	2,664	2,397
Ticket collectors, porters, etc.	18,604	17,158
Guards	11,040	10,373

As soon as the closure decision became known a campaign began to save the railway, some of it perhaps based largely on nostalgia, but with cogent arguments also being put forward in support of the view that the railway had become too important to the operation of the Port for it to be allowed to close. The local press was strongly and volubly in favour of the retention of the railway, and through its various pages a number of different solutions was proposed. One obvious one was that the Mersey Docks and Harbour Board, as the party most likely to suffer from the closure, should take over the operation: had not the Board, after all, been the organisation which had first identified the need for the railway and secured the parliamentary powers for its construction? It should be added that at the date the people of Liverpool had yet to realise that trade in their Port was declining and was no longer the licence to print bottomless pits full of money; it was a period of happy expectations, perhaps summed up in the design then being prepared for the gargantuan new Cunarder Q3. The Dock Board, quite understandably, felt that they were not a railway company, and did not see that they would be justified in spending £2 million to become one, especially as there was at least some prospect of some other body taking over the LOR. This, after all, had been their policy at the time of the building of the railway.

Another leading contender was, of course, British Railways: why should the LOR not

Mobil

Above:
The first section of the overhead structure being demolished just North of Herculaneum in September 1957. *Liverpool Daily Post*

simply be nationalised like most other railways had been? The reason it should not was, in the opinion of the Minister of Transport that it had not been nationalised because it was a purely local undertaking perhaps analogous to a municipal tramway, and this situation was not altered by the unfortunate plight of the company. This left the way open for the suggestion that the railway should be taken over by the City Council. Eventually the Council expressed a willingness to meet a reasonable share of the costs, but it was never likely that they would have been willing to fund the whole of the reconstruction work. Another suggestion which was made was that this issue might be considered as precipitating the question of whether or not there should be a new Merseyside Transport Authority, to co-ordinate all forms of local transport on Merseyside, including the LOR, in much the way that the Merseyside Passenger Transport Executive has since done. This was perhaps the solution most likely to succeed in the financial sense, but it was an idea too far ahead of its time in terms of people's ideas of local government to attract a great deal of support.

It is interesting to note that in December 1955 the *Evening Express* ran its own opinion poll on the future of the railway, asking its readers to vote for one of three options: close the railway and replace it with a Corporation bus service; have the railway taken over and operated by the Corporation; nationalise the railway. Of those who replied, the vast majority favoured the retention of the railway, and of those favouring retention most were of the opinion that nationalisation was the better course. Had the voters been able to foresee the results of the City Engineer's deliberations, together with those of the Transport Department, the majority against buses would probably have been even larger, for in April 1956, four months after the opinion poll, it was revealed that while the resurfacing of the Dock Road to a standard suitable for buses would only cost an estimated £160,000 the carriage of the LOR's traffic would require 55 buses in service with another five spare, 150 drivers and conductors and additional office and workshop staff. Not only this, but the time required by the buses to ply between Dingle and Seaforth & Litherland would be 42min as compared with 31 min on the railway.

At the meeting of shareholders the decision

Below:
Slow-moving traffic like this can never equal the speed of the old LOR. A bus on the new route 1 to replace the trains waits to pull into the Pier Head stop in January 1957. *Ian Allan Library*

was taken to proceed with the "Bill to provide for the closing of the Liverpool Overhead Railway and for the winding up and dissolution of the Liverpool Overhead Railway Company". In the event, the opinion of counsel as to the timing of the passage of the Bill proved to be optimistic, failing to take into account the strength of feelings aroused in favour of retention. In both Lords and the Commons the representatives of the Corporation expressed the view that the railway was an essential element in the operation of the Port, and that chaos, particularly along the Dock Road, would result from its closure. The leader of the City Council, Alderman Jim Braddock, stated that the City would be willing to participate in a rescue operation, but not to effect it single-handed. The Corporation's view was that the Minister of Transport should intervene, a view not shared by the Minister of Transport. (It should, perhaps, be remembered that Alderman Braddock was the leader of the controlling Labour group on the City Council, while the Government was Conservative.) It was pointed out in the Commons that the Corporation's transport services had always competed keenly with the railway and that even at the eleventh hour the Passenger Transport Department had just extended the route of its No. 16 bus to include the stretch between Litherland and Seaford Sands, thus entering into competition with the only short stretch of the LOR which was thus free of competition from buses or trams. This rather nit-picking argument quite missed the point, which was that buses could not form an adequate replacement for the whole of the traffic carried by the railway, and it was not even sound in fact, for the stretch in question belonged to British Railways, not the LOR.

The eventual fate of the Bill in Parliament was not decisive on the central issue of whether or not the railway would close, for while the bill was passed, it was amended in one important detail. The Bill had sought powers to close the service on 30 December 1956 and to commence that demolition of the structure immediately, but this was amended to require that, while the services might cease on the date sought, the structure must be left intact until September 1957, in order to give sufficient time for the Corporation, or indeed any other interested party adequate time to attempt to save the line. A further amendment increased the sum which had to be set aside for severance pay for the employees from £50,000 to £73,000, though it was understood that the

Below:
Rolling stock temporarily left in Herculaneum carriage shed. *C. E. Box*

Company might not be able to meet this sum: the employees would receive three-quarters of the money, then other liabilities to outside parties would be met, then the employees would receive the balance of their money, finally that which remained, if anything, would be divided among the shareholders, which might conceivably amount to as much as £2 per £10 share held.

As the Bill proceeded through Parliament, and particularly when it was becoming clear that it would almost certainly be passed, the efforts of the campaigners to save the Railway became more strenuous. Prominent among these was Graham Page, MP for Crosby who called a meeting of interested parties at the Alexandra Hall, Crosby on 27 July 1956. About the same time the Company offered to provide further negotiating time by continuing to run the service for another six months, until June 1957, if the City Council would meet the additional maintenance costs which would thus be incurred. The Council seems to have waited to see what would happen in Parliament, for the Finance Committee did not consider the offer until a month after the Bill had been passed, and then declined to enter into any such agreement. The Corporation of Bootle had also some local standing in the matter, for although it was not a transport authority a noticeable stretch of the

Left:
Trains waiting to be sold or broken up at Seaforth. *C. E. Box*

Below left:
Carriages being broken up in the Seaforth sheds. *C. E. Box*

Below:
One of the bridges still remaining.

Above:
Demolishing Pier Head station in November 1957. *Liverpool Daily Post*

railway was within the Borough, but it also declined to become involved. The Bill took four days in the committee stages in the House of Lords and seven days in the Commons, finally receiving the Royal Assent on 2 August. The would-be rescuers had not yet given up, for on 28 September Mr Page held another meeting, this time in Liverpool, at which the Secretary of the Company announced that services on the railway would cease on 30 December. Other meetings were held, and other schemes to save the railway produced, including one by Mr L. Beswick, the Secretary of the Cheshire Federation of Ratepayers, who put a great deal of effort into his plan. The final meeting of this kind was held on 25 February 1957, when the railway had been shut nearly two months, and theft and vandalism had already caused extensive damage. It was more or less inevitable that at this meeting it should be resolved that no further action be taken: what is less clear is why events had reached that stage, when very large numbers of people, some of them decidedly influential, had used their best endeavours to save the railway. They were, moreover, assisted by the events of summer 1956 on a wider stage: on October 29th Israel had attacked Egypt and on November 5th an Anglo-French force of considerable size was sent, in what has been termed the last dying twitches of Empire, to the Canal Zone, The result was an oil shortage which necessitated the rationing of vehicle fuel, a state of affairs which people had had a few years to forget about. The prima facie idiocy of scrapping an electric railway at a time of oil shortage could well have been sufficient to save the line, but it was not. To what then do we ascribe its demise? The most probably explanation is quite simply a lack of decision on the part of local politicians, who

appear to have been broadly in sympathy with the Railway, mostly in favour of its retention, and almost without exception unwilling to take the painful decisions which were necessary sequels to the expressions of pious hopes.

Late in November 1956 the statutory notices were posted giving notice of closure at all stations on the LOR and on many on the Southport Line: their text was as follows:

LIVERPOOL OVERHEAD RAILWAY COMPANY

Liverpool Overhead Railway Act, 1956

CESSATION OF SERVICES

Notice is hereby given that under the provisions of the above-mentioned Act the company will after midnight on Sunday, 30th December, 1956, cease to operate railway services for the use of the public. Dated this 9th day of November, 1956.

BY ORDER OF THE BOARD,
HUGH T. NICHOLSON, *Secretary*.

Above:
The structure being removed from above the Dock Railway.

Sunday 30 December 1956 was a dull overcast day with occasional rain: an altogether suitably dismal day for mourning the end of a railway. Visitors had been arriving from all over the country to witness the end of the railway, with traffic heavy all day despite the weather and the fact that it was Sunday. The last trains left simultaneously from Seaforth Sands and Dingle, the down (northbound) train in the charge of Driver Sutcliffe Fawcett, while the up train was driven by Jack Mackey. The trains represented the two kinds of stock in use, the up train being 25-10-27 original stock and the down being made up of the three modernised coaches 1-13-22. Still on duty, though not driving either of the last trains, was Driver Sam Robinson, who had started with the railway in 1907, while

Above:
With the decking cut away only the uprights remain.

Signalman George Bowers, who signalled both of the last trains, had started in 1913.

Both trains were crowded, and each left to the accompaniment of a deafening salute from long lines of fog warning detonators laid on the track, handbells rang and the flashguns of press cameras fragmented the darkness. As the last down train was about to leave Pier Head Station, Driver Fawcett was handed a bouquet of white chrysanthemums, which had been left at the station as a last tribute to the Overhead ''from the Murphys, of Bevington Bush''. Eventually the trains reached their respective destinations, again to the fusillades of detonators which had sent them out on their way. Soon afterwards the traction current was turned off, the familiar two aspect colour light signals were extinguished and eventually the station lights went out, never to be turned on again. A simple, if poignant ceremony at which to lay to rest a railway which, if small in extent had been great in its innovative enterprise, and for most of its life in its sheer will to survive. It was not, perhaps very significant that the last week's operation returned £2,333, as compared with £2,287 for the corresponding week the previous year; instead of £2 million the railway's admirers had, in the end, raised £46.

The following morning the Liverpool Corporation Passenger Transport Department commenced its new service from Dingle to Seaforth with 44 buses. The long-awaited resurfacing of the Dock Road had still not happened, the old surface of diorite setts being not only as slippery as all others of its ilk, but well past the first flush of youth. The result was that the buses avoided the Dock Road so far as possible, travelling via Dingle Lane, Dingle Mount, Beloe Street, Mill Street, St. James' Place, St. James' Street, Park Lane, Canning Place, Strand Street, Goree, Georges Dock Gates, New Quay, King Edward Street, Great Howard Street, Derby Road, Rimrose Road to Seaforth Sands. Only the short portion of this route from Canning Place to King Edward Street lay on what Liverpudlians loosely call the 'Dock Road', the rest of the route lying anything from 150 to 500yds away from the Dock Road. This was not merely an inconvenience to people going to and from work on the Dock Estate; it soon led to stevedoring firms which had previously bought books of pre-paid tickets from the LOR to shift their gangs from one dock to another having to start running buses of their own, which went where they were needed. Dockers going to work were not only treated to a good deal of unaccustomed and doubtless undesired exercise, they were also charged a good deal more for the privilege, for the LOR had offered a third class workman's return ticket, a concession which did

not exist on the buses. The result was that, for example, Dingle to Pier Head return which had been 8d on the railway was 1s 0d by bus, Pierhead to Seaforth Sands went up from 10½d to 1s 2d, while Wapping to Canada rose from 8½d to 1s 0d – and involved a considerable walk at both ends, Brocklebank to Seaforth, while also involving some walking, showed a comparatively modest rise, from 5d to 6d, but at the other end of the scale Huskisson to Seaforth involved a long walk and the fare was doubled from 6d to 1s 0d.

The timings mentioned in Parliament when the Corporation was opposing the bill for closure were substantially improved upon in the schedules announced, and there must remain some suspicion that the timings forecast to Parliament contained a certain element of window-dressing, but on the other hand it must be pointed out that the time allowed after closure – 36min – was, after the common and absurd practice of bus undertakings, the same at all times of the day. Until well into the 1960s congestion on and around the Dock Road was acute throughout the working day (indeed some might have thought it bad enough to justify the building of a railway), with the result that it was totally unrealistic to imagine that buses should not take at least twice as long to cover the route at some times as they would at others.

Above:
Loading up the decking which has already been cut into short lengths ready for the furnace.

Above:
The uprights having been cut to short lengths are loaded for transport to the scrapyard and the furnaces.

The new route was numbered 1, a number which had been blank in the LCPT timetable for some years, with letter suffixes indicating the variants of the basic route: 1a was the designation of buses which continued north beyond Seaforth Sands (at rush hours only), 1b when northbound went only as far as Bank Hall, 1c went to Millers Bridge, 1d to Strand road. Southbound the 1b went to Park Street, the 1c to Pier Head. When, in 1958, the resurfacing of the Dock Road was completed the No. 1 was re-routed south of Pier Head, following the Dock Road to a point near Toxteth Station and then ascending Park Street to complete the trip to Dingle via Grafton Street, Wellington Road and Mill Street. The extra buses put on at rush hours continued to use the original route via Park Lane, St. James' Street and Mill Street, and were newly designated 1a, while number 1e was applied to extras which ran to Litherland. Later the same year the routes were slightly altered at the north end, with north bound buses proceeding via Grove Street and Regent Road (another part of 'The Dock Road') though still returning on Rimrose Road as before. It would not be unfair to LCPT to remark that their fears as the the adequacy of replacing the LOR with bus services were fairly fully justified.

During the first week of 1957 nine trains made their final journey from the Dingle Tunnel where they had been standing to Seaforth Sands to be broken up or sold. It is perhaps ironic to note that these moved in pairs, one train carrying back the crew which had left the other train at Seaforth: this was, of course, because it was more convenient than walking to catch the bus. At Seaforth they joined two trains which had been in the shed there, and all stood in a line, almost buffer to buffer, on the track between Seaforth and Gladstone until July 1957. From South to North they were: Nos 41-2-42, 30-7-14, 27-10-25, 18-5-29, 28-9-26, 16-12-15, 1-13-22, 20-48-6, 7-16-19, 9-10, and 40-3-39. Of these, virtually all were of the modernised type, for by the beginning of 1956 the rebuilding programme had been well advanced, with only Nos 2, 3, 9 and 13 still in more or less 1892 form. Of these No. 2 was destroyed in the fire at Seaforth Sands Station, and No. 9, having been damaged in the fire was somewhat modified. This left Nos 3 and 13 as almost certainly the oldest electric motor coaches at work anywhere in the world. In July work began on breaking up carriages in the shed at Seaforth, a fate escaped by only three of the 54 carriages left; Nos 14 and 7, respectively rebuilt motor and trailer were sold, and No. 3 was saved for eventual inclusion in the then City of Liverpool Museums, (now Merseyside County Museums) where it was put on display in 1970. The body of No. 7 gravitated to use as a temporary building on the premises of a firm of motor car breakers near Seaforth & Litherland Station, whence it was rescued and may be seen at Steamport Museum in Southport.

Within two months of the closure of the line two things had become clear: that there was virtually no prospect of a last-minute rescue of the railway and that extensive theft and vandalism was proceeding. The latter was a serious matter, as it was not only jeopardising the "scrap" value of the undertaking, with station fittings pulled down, gas installations ripped out, electrical equipment smashed and pillaged, but could also have caused significant danger to members of the public for which the Company would have been liable. At Canning and Brunswick fires had been started, and all these incidences of damage, taken together, led the Company to seek, and obtain, the necessary authority to commence demolition immediately without waiting until 30 September as originally required. Tenders were invited for the demolition of the structure and the making good of the land and roadways below. The successful tenderer was George Cohen, Sons & Co. of London, and the contract for the work was signed on 14 May. The time limit for completion of the work contracted was 13 March 1959.

The General Manager, H. Maxwell Rostron relinquished his post on 31 March 1957, and went into practice as a consulting engineer at 13 Rumford Street, but was not long away from the LOR, for he was soon appointed Consulting Engineer to the liquidators, and Engineer for the demolition. Many of the other former employees succeeded in finding employment with British Railways. The sale of various property owned by the Company at both ends of the line, including Dingle Station and tunnel and the Seaforth Carriage Sheds had begun, and proceeds from this and from the demolition contract meant that the feared difficulties in the payment of the full amount of severance pay did not materialise; the final payments were made in August, up to the total of £73,000 stipulated in the Act for closure. There now remained little for the Company to do, and on 30 September 1957 it held its last meeting, at the Chamber of Commerce in Old Hall Street, at which Liquidators were appointed to wind up the Company, in the persons of Hugh Thayer Nicholson, Secretary of the Company and Donald Malcolm Finlayson, Chartered Accountant.

The demolition contractors had not commenced work immediately, despite the Company's concern in February, and the removal of the structure itself did not begin until 23 September 1957, when work started at a point just north of Herculaneum Station. Within the first 6½ working days eight spans had been removed by gangs working with oxy-acetylene cutters, who had also to reduce all the metal to furnace lengths. By early July the following year the whole of the structure between Herculaneum and a point well to the north of Pier Head had gone, together with the 200ft span at the entrance to the tunnel and the three bow girder bridges, so long a feature of the Pier Head area. Of these, the James Street bridge was the last to go, having stood isolated for some time. On Sunday 6 July it was cut apart by oxy-acetylene, with demolition workers visible running along the tops of the bow girders to reach the correct positions for cutting. A considerable crowd of sightseers gather to watch the spectacle of the old landmark being gradually reduced to pieces small enough for mobile cranes to lift down. Many, one suspects, attended sadly, from a sense of duty to witness the passing of an old friend. Before the end of January 1959 the whole of the structure had gone, and reinstatement proceeded soon after.

For many years odd columns of the structure lingered on, set into the walls of warehouses, but many of these fell victim to the improvement of the Dock Road nearly completed by 1982 and many of those which remain may well disappear as the large-scale reclamation works on the South Docks proceed. The same fate may be shared by the stone steps at Herculaneum Dock which led to the bridge to Herculaneum Station, leaving only one substantial piece of evidence on, or rather in, the ground. The tunnel remains intact, with a specialist motor vehicle breaker operating in Dingle Station, now entered from Kedleston Street. The station is still quite recognisable from the photographs of it when still in use, but if this might be considered the tomb of the railway, its headstone is at the other end of the tunnel, where the portal may still be seen, up the rock face at Herculaneum, its inscription still clearly legible.

Appendices

LOR Stations

Seaforth and Litherland
LMSR (later BR) Liverpool-Southport line. Ribble buses for Waterloo, Blundellsands, Crosby and Southport.
Seaforth Sands
Ribble buses for Seaforth, Waterloo, Crosby and Thornton.
Gladstone Dock (opened 1930)
Canadian Pacific Steamships. Alfred Holt (Blue Funnel Line). United States Line. New Zealand Shipping Co.
Alexandra Dock
Furness Withy & Co. Lamport & Holt Ltd. Pacific Steam Navigation Co. Houlder Bros & Co. Donaldson Bros & Co. R.P. Houston & Co. Ellerman Lines. North Mersey goods station (ex-L&YR).
Langton Dock (opened 1896, closed 1906).
Brocklebank Dock
Pacific Steam Navigation Co. Royal Mail Lines Ltd. Houlder Bros & Co. Donaldson Bros & Black Ltd. Langton goods station (ex-LNWR).
Canada Dock
Pacific Steam Navigation Co. Moss Hutchison Line. Elder Dempster Lines. Canada goods station (ex-L&YR).
Huskisson Dock (opened 1896)
Cunard Steamship Co. Ellerman Lines. Sandon goods station (ex-CLC)
Sandon Dock (closed 1896)
Nelson Dock (opened 1896)
Coast Lines Ltd. Great Howard Street goods station (ex-L&YR)
Clarence Dock
Central Electricity Board. Clarence Electric power station. Stanley Dock (only dock on east of LOR). Clyde Shipping Co. Irish & Mersey Line.
Princes Dock
Pier Head
Liverpool Landing Stage. Birkenhead & Wallasey Ferries. Ocean Lines. Isle of Man Steam Packet Co. Liverpool & North Wales Steamship Co. Belfast & Dublin Vessels. Riverside railway station. City Centre. Mersey Tunnel.
James Street
City Centre. Liverpool Landing Stage. Mersey Railway.
Custom House (renamed Canning from 1947)
Lifeboat Training School.
Wapping Dock
British & Continental Steamship Co. Booth Steamship Co. Palm Line Ltd. Park Lane goods station. Liverpool Cathedral.
Brunswick Dock
T & J Harrison. Elder Dempster Lines Ltd. Guinea Gulf Line. Isle of Man Steam Packet Co. Brunswick goods station (ex-CLC). Liverpool Cathedral.
Toxteth Dock
Elder Dempster Lines Ltd.
Herculaneum Dock (new station opened 1896)
Elder Dempster Lines Ltd. Booker Line Ltd. Brunswick mpd (ex-CLC).
Dingle
Sefton Park. Liverpool Cricket Ground. Otterspool Promenade. Buses to Garston Docks.

Station and Distances

Station No.	Station	Station to Station in yds.	Total Miles yds.
1	Seaforth and Litherland	0	– –
2	Seaforth Sands	1,047	– 1,047
3	Gladstone Dock	708	– 1,755
4	Alexandra Dock	782	1 777
5	Langton Dock	300	1 1,077
6	Brockleband Dock	396	1 1,473

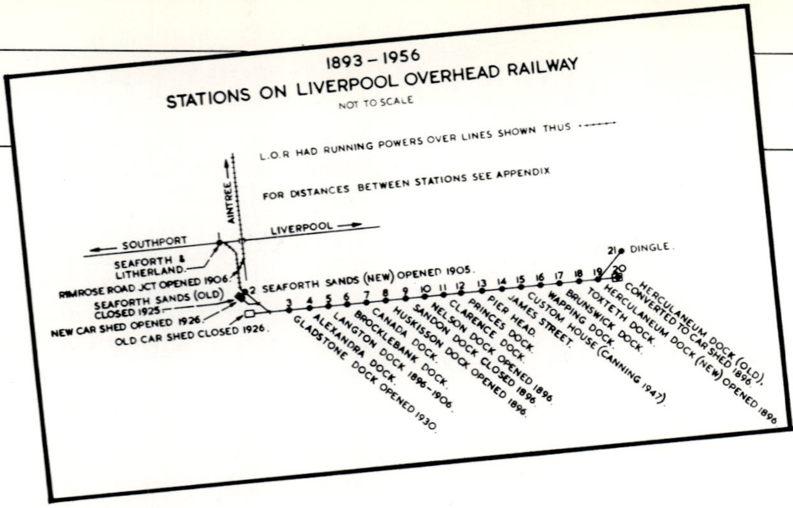

7	Canada Dock	1,068	2 781
8	Huskisson Dock	557	2 1,338
9	Sandon Dock	160	2 1,498
10	Nelson Dock	623	3 361
11	Clarence Dock	446	3 807
12	Princes Dock	1,026	4 73
13	Pier Head	792	4 865
14	James Street	330	4 1,195
15	Custom House (renamed Canning)	274	4 1,469
16	Wapping Dock	808	5 517
17	Brunswick Dock	742	5 1,259
18	Toxteth Dock	701	6 200
19	Herculaneum (new station)	633	6 833
20	Herculaneum (old station)	165	
21	Dingle	1,087	7 160

SPECIFICATIONS OF LOCOMOTIVES

	Lively Polly	Ruston diesel
	0-4-0T	0-4-0
Built by	Kitson & Co. Ltd., Leeds	Ruston & Hornsby Ltd
Date	1893	1947
Length over buffers	15ft 11in	17ft 8in
buffer beams	12ft	
Overall width	8ft 5in	7ft 5in
Height from rail to cab top	9ft 4in	10ft 3⁄8in
Wheel dia	3ft	2ft 6in
Wheelbase	6ft	5ft 2¾in
Cylinders	2 @ 12in by 8in	Four
Boiler dia	2ft 9in	
Heating surface	136.5sq ft	
Grate area	6.4sq ft	
Working pressure	150lbs per sq in	
Tank capacity	200 gall	
Tractive effort	2,720lb	44bhp at 1,000rpm
Weight in working order	10 ton 2cwt	7 ton 10cwt

CHAIRMEN OF LOR 1893-1956

Sir William Bower Forwood, JP
Harvey Cecil Woodward, JP
George Deane Killey, JP
Maxwell Hyslop Maxwell, CBE, JP
George Thompson Phizackerley, OBE
Arthur Thomas Harding
Edmond Gladstone Brownhill, JP
Robert John Hall, JP
J. Edward Jones
Lt. Col. Albert Buckley, CBE, DSO, JP

GENERAL MANAGERS AND ENGINEERS

1893-1908 Stephen Butler Cottrell, MICE, MIMech E
1908-1926 Edward John Neachell, MIMech E, MIEE
1926-1930 William Thomas Dewick Grundy, MInst T
1934-1943 Wilfrid Leonard Box, AMIMech E
1943-1956 Harry Maxwell Rostron, AMIEE

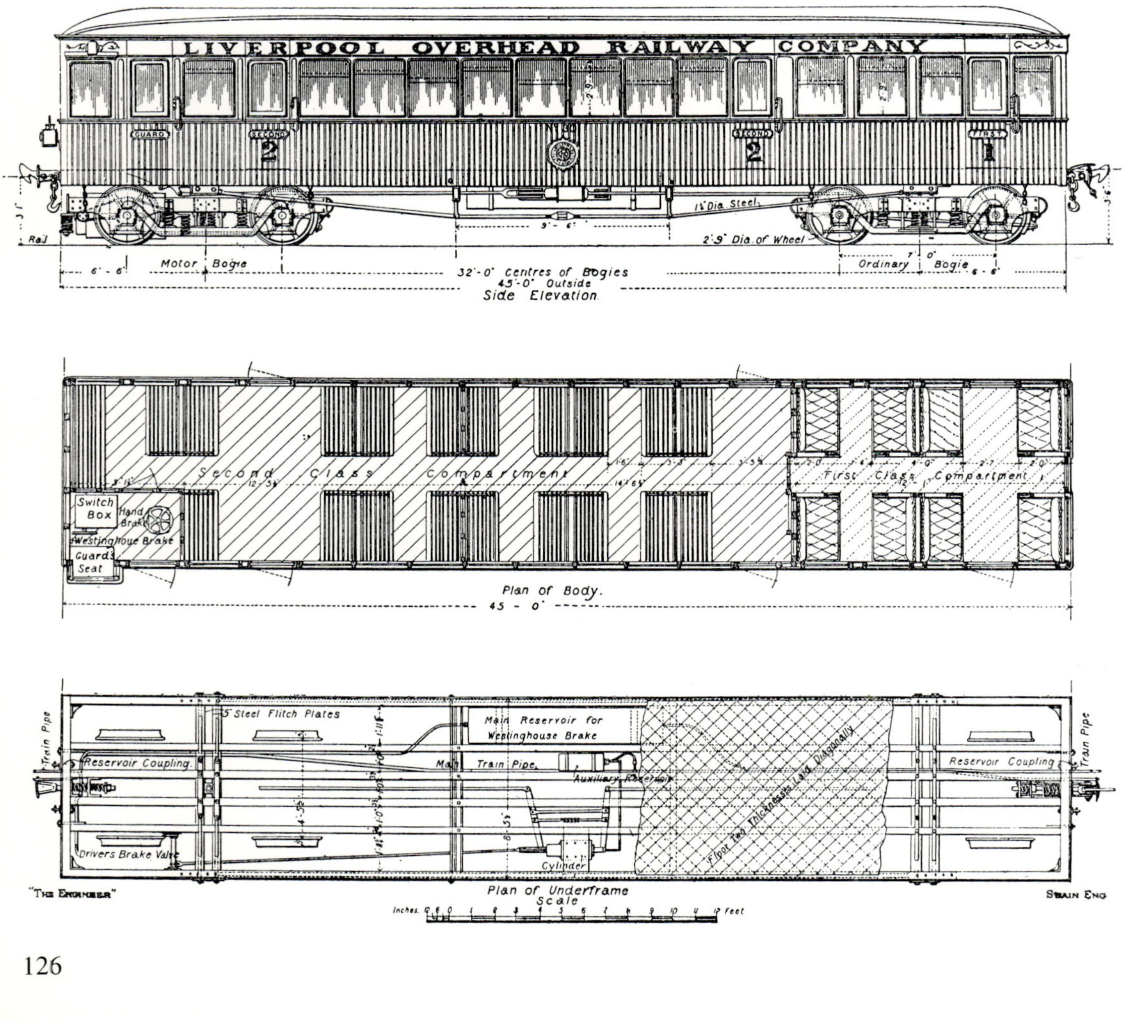